Karen Roark

KID'S LIT

Suggested Activities to Motivate the Teaching of Children's Literature

AUTHOR
K. Sue Bradley

PUBLISHED BY
EDUCATIONAL SERVICE, INC.
P.O.BOX 219
STEVENSVILLE, MICHIGAN 49127

Copyright 1987 ©
EDUCATIONAL SERVICE, INC.
P.O. BOX 219
Stevensville, Michigan 49127
Printed in U. S. A.
ISBN –89273-139-7

TABLE OF CONTENTS

PAGE

UNIT I: WORD RECOGNITION AND VOCABULARY

UNIT II: COMPREHENSION

UNIT III: DICTIONARY AND REFERENCE SKILLS

UNIT IV: CRITICAL THINKING

PAGE

UNIT V: CREATIVE WRITING

UNIT VI: ENCOURAGING INDEPENDENT READING

INTRODUCTION

KID'S LIT is designed to give teachers ideas for activities they can use in their classrooms to involve students with children's literature as they guide students' learning of language arts.

The activities are designed to enhance children's enjoyment and understanding of books. The enjoyment and learning possible through children's literature will contribute to children's desires to want to learn to read, read better or do more reading.

As with other books in the **SPICE** series, **KID'S LIT** merely offers suggestions for teachers. Teachers are encouraged to pick and choose, add to, take away from and delete any activities in the process of tailoring this book to fit the needs of specific classrooms and individual students. This kind of flexibility allows the teacher to adapt the resources in this document to a more individualistic teaching style. It also permits more sensitive attention to the problems and possibilities of particular students.

UNIT I
WORD RECOGNITION AND VOCABULARY

1. DRAW A SOUND (Grades K-3)

A. Purpose: This is an activity to provide practice in using beginning sounds.

B. Materials: Provide a selection of picture books, a shoe box filled with letter cards, paper and pencils.

C. Introduction to the Class: Each child is given a picture book and is instructed to draw a card from the shoe box. The cards the students draw will have letters printed on them. They are to find words in their picture book beginning with the letter they each draw. At the end of a time limit, whoever has the most words wins the game. (It is important to use consonant letters which are more commonly seen in order to give everyone an equal chance.)

2. LISTEN FOR THAT SOUND (Grades K-3)

A. Purpose: To provide practice in hearing specific consonant sounds.

B. Materials: Provide a selection of story titles, paper and pencils.

C. Introduction to the Class: The teacher should write a letter on the chalkboard and the children should practice saying that sound. Then the children should number their papers down the left side of their paper. The teacher then says the name of the book and instructs the students to write ''yes'' next to number one if they hear the sound of the letter on the chalkboard. The students should not see the story title written down. If they do not hear the sound of the letter that is written on the board, they should write ''no'' next to number one. Repeat this exercise with all of the story titles. This is an auditory exercise.

3. BEGINNING CONSONANT RACE (Grades K-3)

A. Purpose: To provide students with repetition of beginning sounds.

B. Materials: Provide a selection of picture books, paper and pencils.

C. Introduction to the Class: Give each child a book. Then write a beginning consonant on the chalkboard. Make sure to give example words which begin with that consonant sound. The students should then be instructed to write down any word they find which begins with the sound on the chalkboard. Set a time limit on this activity. The student who has the most words written down with the correct sound at the end of the time limit wins the game.

D. Variation: Use consonant blends, such as cl, bl, cr, or br, or consonant digraphs, such as sh, th, wh, or ch, instead of beginning consonant sounds.

4. BUILD A WORD (Grades K-3)

A. Purpose: To provide students with practice in word recognition.

B. Materials: Provide poster board cut into one inch squares with letters printed on them and provide a selection of picture books.

C. Introduction to the Class: Give each child fifteen of the one inch squares, five with vowels and ten with consonants. Also give each child a picture book. The students are to use their squares to form words in their picture book. After a set time limit, the student who has used the most letters correctly wins the game.

5. CONFIGURATION MAGIC (Grades K-4)

A. Purpose: To use configuration in decoding words.

B. Materials: Provide strips of poster board (four inches by eight inches) with primary lines drawn on them and also provide pencils.

C. Introduction to the Class: The class should be divided into five groups. Each group is given five picture books with one-word titles. The children are to print the name of each book on a piece of poster board.

Example:

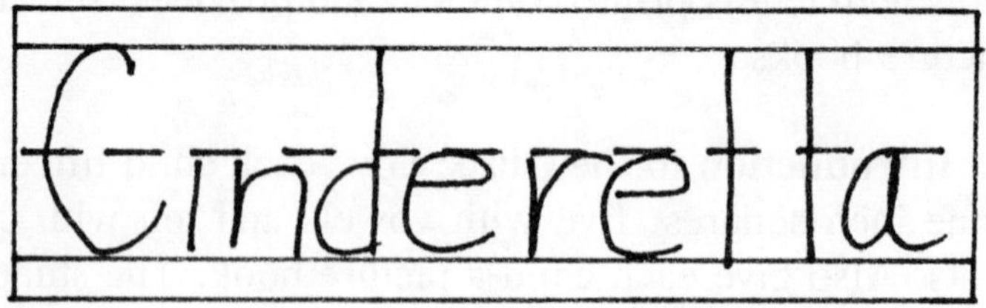

Then the children are to use another piece of poster board to cut out the shape of the word.

Example:

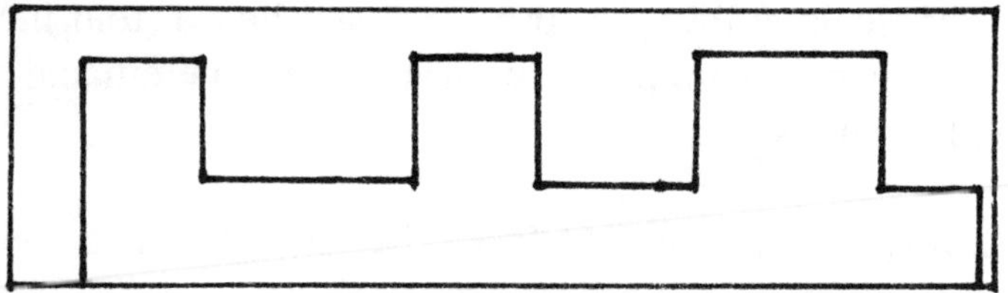

When the cut out piece of poster board is placed over the other piece of poster board, the title is visible. When the children finish this for all five book titles, they trade puzzles with another group and fit the other group's puzzles together. (NOTE: When the primary lines are drawn on the poster board, vertical lines, leaving equal spaces for each letter, should also be drawn.)

6. WORD ENDINGS (Grades 2-4)

A. Purpose: To provide the students with practice in using suffixes.

B. Materials: Provide students with a selection of picture books, paper and pencils.

C. Introduction to the Class: The teacher should discuss suffixes which are added to verbs. Some examples of these are: ful, ing, less, er, ed, s and est. The class is divided into five groups. Each child is given a picture book. Each child is to find a "doing" word and write it on the top of a sheet of paper. Then the students of one group trade papers with the students of another group and complete the following exercise. Each student should add any suffixes which can be used with the word they are given. Not all of the suffixes can be used for every word. After finishing this, each child should read his/her list of words to the class. It may be helpful to write the following example on the board.

<u>   Jump   </u>

Jumps
Jumping
Jumped
Jumper

7. AUDITORY DISCRIMINATION (Grades 1-4)

A. Purpose: To provide students with practice in hearing vowel sounds.

B. Materials: Provide a picture book, a duplicated sheet similar to the one shown and pencils.

Long a	Short a	Long e	Short e	Long i	R con-trolled
Short i	Short o	Long o	Short u	Long u	

C. Introduction to the Class: Begin your presentation by reading a picture book to the class. The teacher should choose some words from the book which would fall under each of the headings on the duplicated sheet. After reading the book, the teacher reads the words chosen to the class and the students must write the words under the proper headings. (With younger children, it may be necessary to do this exercise as a group on the chalkboard.)

8. LONG AND SHORT VOWELS (Grades 2-4)

A. Purpose: To give children practice in reading words with long and short vowel sounds.

B. Materials: Provide the children with a selection of picture books, paper and pencils.

C. Introduction to the Class: Instruct the children to write down all the one syllable words that they can find in their books. The books should be picture books with only a small amount of writing. When the students complete this, have them underline short vowel one syllable words with a blue crayon and long vowel one syllable words with a red crayon. Repeat this exercise by having the children trade books with someone. Have them compare their answers.

9. VOWEL DISCRIMINATION (Grades 2-4)

Hat	Nut	Go	Bet	Hot
Far	Turn	Word	Cup	Game
Kite	Goat	Gate	Her	Hit
Meet	Box	Cute	Fir	Cat

A. Purpose: To provide students with practice in using vowels.

B. Materials: Strips of paper, a selection of picture books, pencils and a prepared duplicated sheet will be needed.

C. Introduction to the Class: Give each child a picture book and instruct the students to find words with the same vowel sound as on the duplicated sheet. The first child to cover all the boxes with words to match the vowel sounds wins the game. Repeat this exercise for additional practice for the students.

10. CONTROLLED R VOWEL SOUND COVER UP (Grades 2-4)

A. Purpose: To provide students with practice in identifying vowel sounds with controlled R.

B. Materials: A selection of picture books, strips of paper, pencils and a set of cards using vowel sounds with controlled R (er, ir, or, ur) will be needed.   Example:

er	ir	ur
ur	er	or
ur	ir	or

C. Introduction to the Class: Tell each student to select a partner. Every child has a picture book, but two children share a card such as the one shown. When the teacher says ''go'', the children will look for words with the R controlled vowel, write them on strips of paper and cover the appropriate box on the card (As is done in Bingo). The first group that covers its card wins the game. They must read the words aloud to the class before they officially are proclaimed to be the winners. Repeat this game for extra practice. Example words with R controlled vowels are as follows:

burn	word	bird	her
turn	work	fir	serve
curve	worm	first	nerve

11. SYLLABLES (Grades 2-4)

A. Purpose: To identify the number of syllables contained in different words.

B. Materials: A prepared worksheet similar to the following will be needed.

C. Introduction to the Class: Give each child a picture book and a copy of the prepared duplicated sheet. The children are to locate words with one, two, three and four syllables and write them under the proper headings on the duplicated sheet. A time limit should be set. Whoever has the most words correctly placed at the end of the set time limit wins the game. The children should take turns reading some of their words and clapping out the syllables with the class.

<table>
<tr><td colspan="4" style="text-align:center">How Many Syllables ?</td></tr>
<tr><td>1</td><td>2</td><td>3</td><td>4</td></tr>
<tr><td></td><td></td><td></td><td></td></tr>
</table>

12. MORE SYLLABLES (Grades 2-4)

A. Purpose: To identify one, two and three syllable words.

B. Materials: Provide a selection of picture books, paper and pencils.

C. Introduction to the Class: Give each student a book. Next instruct them to list all of the one syllable words from the first page of the story, the two syllable words from the second page and the three syllable words from the third page. After completing this, have them trade books with another student. The same procedure should be followed with the new book. When this has been completed, the students are to compare papers.

13. LEAVE OUT A LETTER (Grades 3-5)

A. Purpose: To give students practice in recognizing partially completed words.

B. Materials: A selection of picture books, paper, pencils and 3 x 5 cards will be needed.

C. Introduction to the Class: Provide a book and a 3 x 5 card for each student. The student is to write ten words on the card, leaving out one letter in each word. (Example - Hap_y) After writing out the words, the student is to trade cards with someone and then try to fill in the letter to complete the words on that card. The student may use the book if necessary. This activity can be made more difficult by leaving out more than one letter in each word.

14. PREFIXES AND SUFFIXES (Grades 2-4)

A. Purpose: To provide practice in using prefixes and suffixes.

B. Materials: Provide a list of prefixes and suffixes, paper, pencils and picture books.

C. Introduction to the Class: Select some picture books that have text containing words with prefixes and suffixes. Next write a list of prefixes and suffixes on the chalkboard. Refer to the following sample list:

re-	sub-	-able	-est
dis-	pre-	-er	-ship
un-	pro-	-ful	-or
in-		-ic	-ness
con-		-ish	-ment
mis-		-ist	-less

After preparing the chalkboard, give each child a book and instruct the class to write down five words from their books that contain these prefixes and suffixes. After finding the five words, they are to write sentences using these five words.

15. BLEND WAGON TRAIN (Grades 2-5)

A. Purpose: To associate letter blends with their corresponding sounds.

B. Materials: Provide duplicated pictures of a wagon for each child, a selection of picture books, paper and pencils. Each wagon should have a blend written on it before the pictures are given to the children.

C. Introduction to the Class: Give each student a picture of a wagon similar to the one shown. The students are to use a book to locate words with the blend they have on their wagon. After finding such words, they are to write them on their wagon. At the end of a specified time period, whoever has the most words with their blend wins the race. At the end of the game, the students select a partner and read their words to each other. A list of blends follow:

bl,   cl,   fl,   gl,   pl,   sl
br,   cr,   dr,   fr,   gr,   pr
sk,   sm,   sc,   sn,   sp,   st
scr,   spl,   spr,   shr,   thr   str

D. Variation: The same game could be played using any of the following final consonant blends.

ct,   ft,   ld,   lf,   lm,   pt
nt,   nk,   nd,   mp,   lp,   lt
rm,   rl,   rd,   rk,   sk,   sp   st

16. SUBSTITUTION OF LETTERS (Grades 2-5)

A. Purpose: To provide practice in using consonants and to improve the students' comprehension of sentences.

B. Materials: Provide paper, pencils and a selection of picture books with a limited amount of text in them.

C. Introduction to the Class: The teacher is to read the first sentence of a picture book, changing one word in the sentence by changing a beginning consonant sound. Example:

Tommy did not _b_ike to clean his room.

The children are to identify the incorrect word and fix it. After going through the book, have the students select a partner and follow the same procedure. The two children are to take turns changing a sentence and calling on their partners to fix it.

17. MAKE THE PLURAL FORM (Grades 2-4)

A. Purpose: To provide students with practice in making plurals.

B. Materials: Provide a selection of picture books, paper and pencils.

C. Introduction to the Class: Each child is given a picture book and is instructed to write down fifteen words from the book which name things. Then they should choose a partner and trade words with him or her. The children are to make the plural form of all of their partner's words. After completing this, the children should take turns reading and spelling the plurals to the class.

18. USING DESCRIBING WORDS (Grades 1-5)

A. Purpose: To expand students' vocabulary through the use of adjectives.

B. Materials: A picture book will be needed.

C. Introduction to the Class: The teacher will read a picture book to the students. A picture book should be selected which has several very well developed characters, with different character traits. The teacher will write the character's names on the chalkboard and the students will try to come up with words which describe the different characters. The teacher will write the describing words under the proper headings on the chalkboard similar to the following (from Hansel and Gretel):

Hansel	Gretel	Stepmother	Father	Witch
shy	shy	mean	weak	wicked
quiet	quiet	horrible	kind	terrible
helpful	afraid	ugly		ugly

19. SIGHT WORD PRACTICE (Grades 2-4)

A. Purpose: To provide practice in using small words which are not phonetically decodable.

B. Materials: A selection of picture books, paper and pencils will be needed.

C. Introduction to the Class: Give a picture book to each child. Next, write ten words on the chalkboard. These should be frequently used words which cannot be decoded phonetically. The children are to find five of these words in sentences in their books. After finding the words, they are to copy the sentence on their paper. When everyone is finished, the children should take turns reading their sentences. A sample word list follows:

to	new	walk	out
do	you	there	of
are	your	where	eight
put	saw	what	who
once	was	into	

20. USING PRONOUNS (Grades 3-5)

A. Purpose: To ensure understanding of the use of pronouns in place of the subject and to improve comprehension.

B. Materials: A selection of picture books, paper and pencils will be needed.

C. Introduction to the Class: Discuss the use of the pronouns, he, she, it, and they in the place of the subject of a sentence. Read the first page of a picture book to the class and write all the pronouns on the chalkboard. Next, write the noun to which each pronoun refers next to that pronoun. For example:

> it-ball
> he-Sam
> she-Susan

Continue through the book, following the same procedure. After going through the book as a class, have the students repeat the activity independently.

21. DRAW A WORD (Grades K-4)

A. Purpose: To develop vocabulary.

B. Materials: Provide a selection of picture books, paper, pencils, a shoe box and 3 x 5 cards.

C. Introduction to the Class: Each student should be given a book and three 3 x 5 cards. The students are instructed to think of the words in the story which name something. Write one naming word (noun) on each card. Put the cards in the shoe box and let each child draw one. The children are to illustrate the word and write the word below the picture. After everyone is finished, share the pictures with the class.

22. VOCABULARY PRACTICE (Grades 1-3)

A. Purpose: To learn categorizing and to enrich vocabulary.

B. Materials: A picture book will be needed.

C. Introduction to the Class: The teacher reads a picture book to the class, stopping at the end of each page to discuss specific vocabulary. Two headings should be written on the board that say, "Someone may feel", and "Someone may use".   Example:

Someone may feel	Someone may use
proud	cable car
warm	building
cozy	paper sack
kind	bridge
terrible	traffic signal
gentle	umbrella
lucky	shop

(Example taken from, <u>Fly High, Fly Low</u>, by Don Freeman)

23. VOCABULARY (Grades 4-5)

A. Purpose: To develop vocabulary.

B. Materials: Provide a selection of non-fiction books, paper and pencils.

C. Introduction to the Class: Each student should be given a book and instructed to find five words in the book which they don't know. They are to write these five words on a piece of paper. Next, they are to look up these words in the dictionary, write definitions for each word and then use each word in a sentence. When this is completed, they are to share information with another student.

24. VOCABULARY ENRICHMENT (Grades 3-6)

A. Purpose: To enrich vocabulary.

B. Materials: A variety of books will be needed.

C. Introduction to the Class: The teacher should prepare a list of vocabulary words, using action words and descriptive words. After the lists have been prepared, the students are asked to choose three vocabulary words. They are to find one book which relates to each of their vocabulary words. For example, using the vocabulary word ''exciting'', a student might choose the book, ''Swiss Family Robinson''. In class discussion, the students are to tell how the book relates to the word. Using short stories, rather than books might be more successful with older students. A sample word list follows. The word lists can be changed to fit any grade level.

exciting	boring	happy
interesting	sad	thrilling
beautiful	ugly	sleek
tremendous	bubbly	adventuresome
unbelievable	awful	listen

camp	discover	explore
laugh	cry	sing
run	study	compete
hurry	love	hate
frighten		

(Notice the mixture of verbs and adjectives.)

25. GUESS ME (Grade K-8)

A. Purpose: To motivate interest in a particular book.

B. Materials: Prepared duplicated copies of the game will be needed.

C. Introduction to the Class: Instruct the students to figure out the name of the book, or a character in the book, by working out the letter puzzle on the line provided.

My first letter is in boy, but not in Bob   _______
My second letter is in due, and also in see   _______
My third is in run, but not in sun   _______
My fourth is in sit and also in not   _______
My fifth is in call but not in cat   _______
My sixth is in gave, and also in lone   _______

My first is in toy, but not in boy   _______
My second is in ham and also in hit   _______
My third is in he, but not in ho   _______

My first is in pit, but not in pig   _______
My second is in gun, but not in gone   _______
My third is in try, and also in car   _______
My fourth is in rat, but not in ran   _______
My fifth is in all and also in tell   _______
My last is in eat, but not in at   _______

Answer: Yertle the turtle

26. SYNONYMS AND ANTONYMS (Grades 2-5)

A. Purpose: To provide practice in using synonyms and antonyms.

B. Materials: A prepared duplicated sheet with the titles of books on it and pencils will be needed.

C. Introduction to the Class: The students should be instructed to write one synonym and one antonym for each underlined word. A sample duplicated sheet is shown:

	Synonym	Antonym
The <u>Boy</u> Who Tried to Cheat Death	Lad	Girl
You Will Live <u>Under</u> the Sea	Below	Above
The <u>Funny</u> Thing	Amusing	Sad
Mr. Charlie, the Fireman's <u>Friend</u>	Pal	Enemy
Short and <u>Tall</u>	Big	Short
The Boy Who <u>Fooled</u> the Giant	Tricked	Was Fair To

The duplicated sheet can be changed to fit any level. The last example shows that sometimes it is necessary to use more than one word in a synonym or antonym.

27. ANTONYMS (Grades 2-5)

A. Purpose: To provide practice in using antonyms.

B. Materials: A selection of picture books, paper and pencils will be needed.

C. Introduction to the Class: Each child should be given a picture book and instructed to write down ten words which describe something. Each child selects a partner and trades word lists with him/her. The students are to write opposites for each of their partner's words. When everyone is finished, the children should take turns reading some of their words with their opposites.

28. CONTRACTIONS (Grades 2-5)

A. Purpose: To match contractions to their corresponding words.

B. Materials: Provide a selection of picture books, pencils and paper.

C. Introduction to the Class: Each child should be given a picture book and instructed to locate some contractions or their corresponding words in his book. (A child can use either do not or don't.) They are to write these words on their paper with the corresponding contraction or group of words next to it. A time limit should be set. The student with the most contractions with their corresponding words at the end of the time limit wins the game.

29. FIT THE STORY TITLES IN THE PUZZLE (Grades 3-5)

A. Purpose: To give students practice in working with puzzles.

A sample puzzle follows:

B. Materials: Pencils and a prepared duplicated sheet with the puzzle on it will be needed.

C. Introduction to the Class: The teacher should write the name of eight or ten books on the chalkboard. The children are to fit the titles into the puzzle given to them.

UNIT II
COMPREHENSION

1. PICTURE CLUES FOR READING (Grades K-3)

A. Purpose: To facilitate comprehension by reading pictures.

B. Materials: A set of picture books, paper and pencils will be needed.

C. Introduction to the Class: The teacher shows the pictures of a picture book without reading the story. From the pictures, the children must decide what kind of book it is. The following statements should be written on the board:

> It is scary.
> It is funny.
> It is sad.

(These are just examples, others may be used.)

After doing this activity as a group, have each student select a book and a partner. Each child shows a book to the partner and his/her partner decides what kind of book it is. Share some with the class, having the students give some reason for saying the book was funny, or sad, etc.

2. MATCH THE WORD TO THE PICTURE (Grades K-3)

A. Purpose: To develop picture comprehension.

B. Materials: One 3 ft. by 3 ft. board, burlap, felt squares, yarn and poster board will be needed.

C. Introduction to the Class: The teacher should prepare for this activity by covering the board with burlap and cutting felt squares into figures representing something in the story. Also, a word or phrase describing the word should be written on the poster board. The children should be instructed to independently match the word or phrase with the picture by using the yarn to connect the word to the figure. The board can be left up with the phrases and figures changed regularly.

3. PICTURE CONTEXT CLUES (Grades K-3)

A. Purpose: To learn to use context clues to decode words.

B. Materials: Provide a picture book, pencils and a duplicated sheet similar to the one shown.

C. Introduction to the Class: The teacher should copy a paragraph from a picture book on a duplicated sheet, leaving out the nouns.

Example:

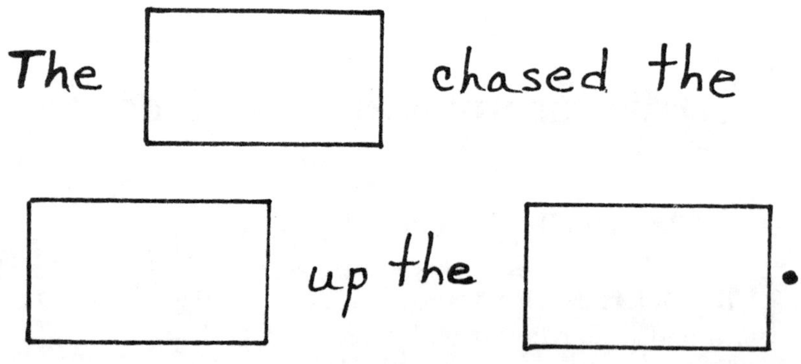

The children are to draw pictures in the boxes provided to make the sentences sensible. When the activity is completed, the teacher should read the picture book to the children.

4. WORK OUT WORDS (Grades 1-8)

A. Purpose: To use context clues to work out words.

B. Materials: A picture book or short story should be chosen that the class has not heard before.

C. Introduction to the Class: Read the story to the class stopping in the middle of each sentence, asking the class to guess what word comes next. A game can be played using this technique. Instead of saying the word, have the children write it. At the end of the story, correct the papers together. Each word counts one point and the child with the most points wins the game. At the close of the activity, point out that this is the technique of working out words using context clues. Older children can understand how this can be useful in their individual reading.

5. LISTEN FOR THE SENTENCE THAT DOES NOT FIT (Grades 2-5)

A. Purpose: To pick out the sentence that does not fit.

B. Materials: A picture book will be needed.

C. Introduction to the Class: The teacher should read one page of the picture book, adding a sentence which has

nothing to do with the story. The children should listen for
the wrong sentence and take turns repeating it to the class.
Example from <u>Little Black, A Pony</u>, by Walter Farley:

''When I was little, I had a pony. I called him Little Black.
The sun is hot today. He was my very, very good friend.''

At the end of the activity, the teacher should read the book
to the class without interruption.

6. MAKE IT MAKE SENSE (Grades 2-5)

A. Purpose: To use context to figure out missing words.

B. Materials: Provide a picture book and chalkboard
space.

C. Introduction to the Class: Copy a paragraph out of
the picture book on the chalkboard, leaving out every fifth
word. Read each sentence to the children, having them fill
in the spaces with words which make sense. Choose several
children to read the whole paragraph. When this activity is
completed, the teacher should read the paragraph from the
book. In class discussion, compare the two paragraphs. After
the discussion, finish reading the story to the children.

7. I'M THINKING OF A CHARACTER (Grades 1-5)

A. Purpose: To develop language skills.

B. Materials: A picture book will be needed.

C. Introduction to the Class: The teacher should read a picture book or a short story to the class. The one used should have a number of characters. The teacher starts the game by saying, ''I'm thinking of a character that I will describe to you. You must guess my character.'' The teacher uses only one word to describe the character. After a wrong guess, the teacher gives another describing word. The children continue to guess until someone guesses the correct character. The person who guesses correctly becomes the leader and follows the teacher's example.

8. MAKE SENTENCES (Grades 2-4)

A. Purpose: To make sentences make sense.

B. Materials: Poster board which is cut into squares will be needed.

C. Introduction to the Class: The teacher should use a picture book to copy some sentences on the poster board squares. Either the beginning, middle or ending parts of the sentences should be printed on the squares. Each student is given all three parts of one sentence. They are to put the sentences in order with the subject first, then the action word and finally the end of the sentence. They will read their sentence to the class after putting it in the correct order. To finish the activity the teacher should read the picture book to the students.

9. END THE SENTENCE (Grades 2-4)

A. Purpose: To use the context of sentences to finish them.

B. Materials: Provide a picture book, a duplicated sheet made up of sentences from the picture book with the ending omitted and pencils.

C. Introduction to the Class: The teacher should make a duplicated sheet, copying some sentences from a picture book. The ending of each sentence must be omitted. The students are to finish the sentences. When this is completed, the teacher should read the picture book to the class stressing the sentences on the duplicated sheeet. The children are to compare their answers to the book's text.

10. STORY BOOK CONCENTRATION (Grades 2-5)

A. Purpose: To match story titles.

B. Materials: Cards with the titles of books written on them will be needed.

C. Introduction to the Class: All the cards are placed face down on the floor, similar to the following example:

Pairs of cards should have the same book title on them. The children, in turn, flip over two cards trying to make a match. If a match is made, the player keeps the two cards and draws two more cards. The player can continue as long as he continues to make matches. The game is over when all the cards are gone. The player with the most cards wins the game.

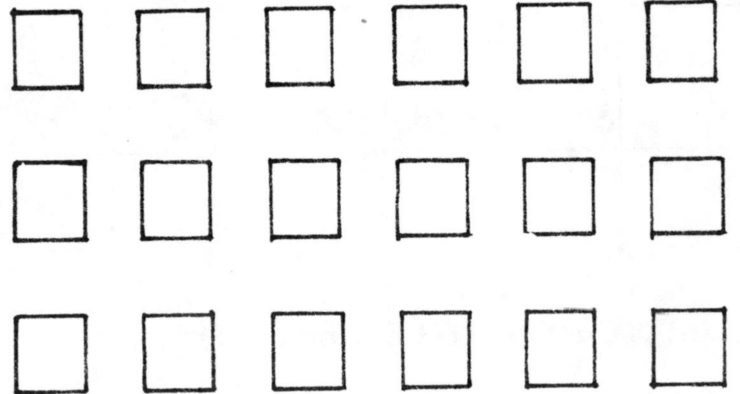

11. HOLIDAY BOOKS (Grades 2-5)

A. Purpose: To categorize and use the title to enhance comprehension.

B. Materials: A selection of picture books or short stories pertaining to different holidays will be needed.

C. Introduction to the Class: The teacher should write the following on the chalkboard:

The teacher reads the name of each book and the group decides, by hearing the title only, which holiday is depicted in the story. The teacher then should write it under the proper heading. Each student then should be given a story to read. After the story is read, each student should report to the class as to whether or not the story was placed under the proper heading. If it was incorrect, then it should be corrected.

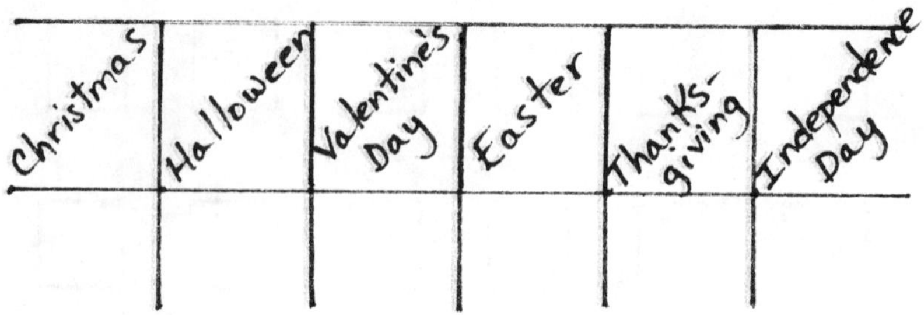

12. MATCH THE TITLE (Grades 3-5)

A. Purpose: To match the title of a book to a sentence describing it.

B. Materials: A selection of very well-known books, paper and pencils will be needed.

C. Introduction to the Class: The teacher chooses twelve well-known books from the library and places them along the chalk tray so that everyone can see them all. Then each student should be given a duplicated sheet of phrases describing the books. Refer to the following example:

A wolf blows a house down. (<u>Three Little Pigs</u>)

A pumpkin changes into a coach. (<u>Cinderella</u>)

Seven little men help a young lady. (<u>Snow White</u>)

A boy climbs a tall plant. (<u>Jack and the Beanstalk</u>)

A little girl helps herself to some porridge. (<u>The Three Bears</u>)

13. WHO'S TALKING? (Grades 1-5)

A. Purpose: To improve reading comprehension.

B. Materials: A picture with a lot of conversation will be needed.

C. Introduction to the Class: The teacher should read a picture book to the class. This book should be mostly conversation. After reading the story, the teacher should reread some sentences which are parts of a conversation. The children are to take turns naming the character who is speaking.

14. WHAT'S HE SAYING? (Grades 2-5)

A. Purpose: To use picture clues to enhance comprehension and to introduce the use of quotation marks.

B. Materials: A selection of picture books, drawing paper and crayons will be needed.

C. Introduction to the Class: Each student should select a story to read. Next, they should choose a character to draw and include a caption next to him/her. Refer to the example shown below:

15. LITERATURE BEE (Grades 4-6)

A. Purpose: To gain a better understanding of various literature books.

B. Materials: Provide scoring materials, a list of questions, paper and pencils.

C. Introduction to the Class: Before this game can be conducted successfully, several books should have been read and discussed by the class. The main idea of each book should be stressed. Then the children must become familiar with the rules of the literature bee. Once the preparation for this activity has been completed, the class should be divided into two teams with an equal number of members on each. The teacher proceeds to ask questions concerning the characters, plots or particular incidents in the books. The teams stand in two lines and each member takes a turn answering a question. The teacher asks one team member a question, and then switches to the first member of the other team. If a team member answers the question correctly, that team gets one point. If it is answered incorrectly, the team gets no point. The team with the greatest number of points after every member of both teams has been asked a question is the winner.

16. GRAB BAG (Grades 3-6)

A. Purpose: To create interest in books.

B. Materials: Provide a grab bag full of names of books, the books corresponding to these titles, paper and pencils.

C. Introduction to the Class: The children should each grab a book name from the grab bag. They are then directed to write a story about the title. It should be a book which they have not read before. When the children are finished writing their stories, they are given the corresponding book to read. Choose several children to share their stories with the class.

17. WHERE DOES YOUR STORY TAKE PLACE? (Grades 4-8)

A. Purpose: To motivate the students' interest in reading.

B. Materials: A world map, pins, yarn, string or ribbon and shelf paper will be needed.

C. Introduction to the Class: Using an opaque projector, project the outline of a world map on shelf paper and have the students trace it. Fasten the shelf paper to the wall or bulletin board. Make sure to leave enough space around the border to provide for illustrations. Each child should read a book and is encouraged to select a character or incident in the story to illustrate. Use string, colored yarn or ribbon to connect the illustration with the country in which the story takes place. Straight pins might be used to tack the ends of the yarn in place. Encourage the students to continue to add to this story map of the world.

18. LIVE A STORY (Grades K-3)

A. Purpose: To note fantasy in literature.

B. Materials: The book entitled Where the Wild Things Are by Maurice Sendak, small paper sacks, paper plates and crayons or felt pens will be needed.

C. Introduction to the Class: Read the book, Where the Wild Things Are, to the class. It is great to use around Halloween time to get small children used to seeing masks and scary costumes before they go trick-or-treating. After reading the story and discussing the characters, the children are to select a character to portray. The entire class can be used in acting out the story. Some could portray the wild things, some trees and plants and one could be Max, one his mother and one his dog.

19. PLAY A ROLE (Grades 3-6)

A. Purpose: To encourage reading.

B. Materials: Numerous books should be available to allow for choice.

C. Introduction to the Class: Each student should assume the identity of a character in a book or short story he/she has read. They are to write letters to different members of the class. In the letters, they will share the experiences of the character or use their imagination to tell something about "themselves," which was not specifically stated in the story. The letters can be displayed on a bulletin board after they are exchanged. This activity will get students interested in books or stories they have not yet read.

20. DRESS-UP (Grades 1-5)

A. Purpose: To invoke students interest in various books.

B. Materials: Clothes will be needed to portray the student's chosen character.

C. Introduction to the Class: A number of books or short stories should be read to the children prior to attempting this activity. After reading for preparation, the children are instructed to bring clothes to portray any character in any story they have heard in class. This can be done like a show-and-tell period. The class may ask only "yes" or "no" questions to determine what character is being portrayed. After a set number of questions, depending on the maturity of the group and the number of books read, the class is considered stumped and the character wins. Another possibility could be to have the dressed-up character tell something about the book and the students guess the name.

21. BUILD A WORM (Grades 3-5)

A. Purpose: To encourage outside reading.

B. Materials: Provide books, colored construction paper, scissors and a felt pen.

C. Introduction to the Class: Begin by cutting the construction paper into 8 inch circles. Give each child one circle to form the worm's face. Instruct the children to read books outside of class and as a student finishes a book, he/she is given another circle. The title and the author of the book should be written on the circle. Every child's worm face should be displayed on the wall and each student adds another section to the worm when he/she finishes a book.

22. THE BOOK TELEVISION (Grades 3-6)

A. **Purpose:** To make oral reports more exciting.

B. **Materials:** Shelf paper, boxes and sticks will be needed.

C. **Introduction to the Class:** Divide the class into groups of four students who will read the same book. After the students read the book, they will write a summary of the book. From the summary, they will get ideas to draw on shelf paper. When the drawings are completed, the paper is rolled up in the form of a scroll with sticks at each end. The paper and sticks can be placed at each end of a box to make a television type viewer. While one student gives the oral report, the others turn the sticks to unfold the story. An illustration of the viewer follows:

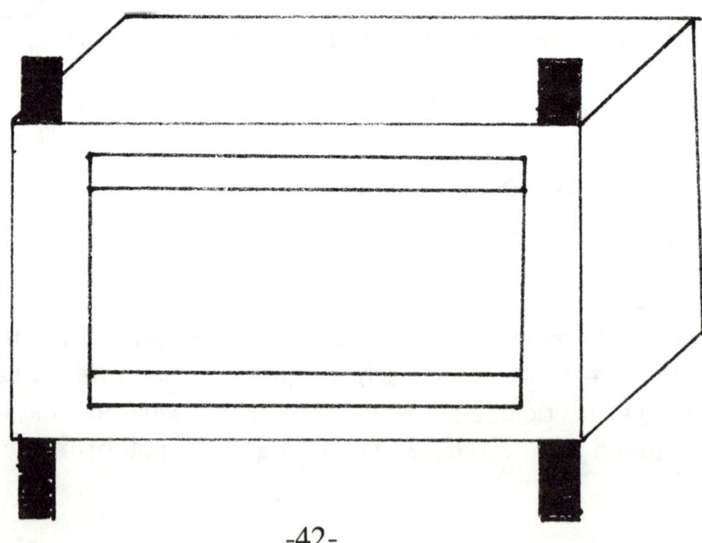

23. PICTURES AND EMOTIONS (Grades 3-5)

A. Purpose: To show children how pictures affect the comprehension of a story.

B. Materials: Provide a picture book, paper and pencils.

C. Introduction to the Class: Choose a picture book which contains pictures with strong emotional content. Show one picture and ask questions similar to the following and discuss them in class:

1. What do you think happened in this picture?

2. Why is the little boy sad?

3. Who do you think might come to help him?

4. Do you think his problems will be solved? How?

5. What do you think caused his problem?

After doing this in class, choose another book to use in repeating the activity. Display one picture to the class, being careful to select a book which is unfamiliar to the students. Instruct the students to think about this list of questions and write a paragraph about the picture. Share the paragraphs in class.

24. EMOTIONS (Grades K-2)

A. Purpose: To show how a reader's voice can change to fit the feelings of a character.

B. Materials: Provide several children's books whose themes emphasize different emotions.

C. Introduction to the Class: Before presenting the story to the class, the teacher should read the story and let his voice reflect the moods of the characters as they react to incidents in the story.

As the teacher is reading, he/she should periodically interrupt the story and ask how a character feels at that moment. Provide the children with opportunities to act out the story. Examples of books to select dealing with specific feelings are as follows:

1. Love - Viereck, Phillip, <u>Let Me Tell You About My Dad</u>

    Gag, Wanda, <u>Millions of Cats</u>

2. Fear - Gay, Zhenya, <u>Who's Afraid</u>
   Steig, William, <u>Sylvester and the Magic Pebble</u>

3. Loyalty - Daughtery, James, <u>Andy and the Lion</u>

25. CHARACTER STUDY (Grades 3-8)

A. Purpose: To provide practice in critical thinking by comparing and contrasting two characters.

B. Materials: A selection of novels, duplicated sheets and pencils will be needed.

C. Introduction to the Class: The students are to read a novel and choose two characters for a follow-up study. A simple form can be duplicated and given to the students to give them an idea of where to start. An example follows:

	(Mary) Character's Name	(Tom) Character's Name
Home		
Personality		
Appearance		
Hobbies		
Responsibilities		
Age		

26. HAVE A PUPPET SHOW (Grades 1-3)

A. Purpose: To introduce students to puppet shows.

B. Materials: Provide a picture book, crayons or markers, paper sacks and socks.

C. Introduction to the Class: Read the story to the class. Discuss the setting. Ask questions such as the following:
1. "If you were going to put on a play, what would you want in the scenery?
2. Do we need buildings to show a city or do we need trees to show a forest?"

Supervise the children in setting up the puppet stage.

Show samples of puppets made from paper sacks and old socks. Give a short demonstration of a puppet show to give the children an idea of what they will be doing. Divide the class into groups of six. Second or third graders might decide to do a different story than the one presented in class but use the same setting and puppets.

27. COMPARE AND CONTRAST (Grades 3-8)

A. Purpose: To stimulate critical thinking and provide practice in finding likenesses and differences.

B. Materials: Provide a duplicated sheet like the example shown, pencils and books.

C. Introduction to the Class: The students are instructed to find two books on the same topic. You may want to work closely with your school librarian in the selection of books. After reading both books, the student is to tell how the books are similar and different. This can be done orally or in written form.

COMPARISON	TITLE	TITLE
Author		
Number of Characters		
Main Theme		
Setting		

28. DISCOVERING THE SENSES (Grades 3-8)

A. Purpose: To develop vocabulary and provide practice in classification.

B. Materials: A selection of books, paper and pencils will be needed.

C. Introduction to the Class: The students are instructed to read their book looking for words which specifically provide sensory impressions. They are to divide their paper into four sections as follows:

Touch	Taste	Smell	Hearing
smooth rough	sour sweet	fragrant spicy	quiet faint

The sensory words are placed in the appropriate columns. The student chooses a partner with whom to share his/her list of words and the partner is to write a story using as many of these words as possible.

29. COULD IT HAPPEN? (Grades 1-4)

A. Purpose: To distinguish between fact and fancy.

B. Materials: A picture book, paper and pencils will be needed.

C. Introduction to the Class: The children should number their papers down the left side of the page. The teacher then reads a sentence from a picture book. The children are to write ''yes'' if it could happen, or ''no'' if it could not happen. Discuss the sentences in class.

30. COULD IT BE TRUE? (Grades 2-4)

A. Purpose: To match phrases which could be true about certain stories.

B. Materials: Provide several picture books, a prepared duplicated sheet similar to the example and pencils.

C. Introduction to the Class: The teacher should read several picture books to the children and also prepare a duplicated sheet similar to the following:

Hansel and Gretel	The Three Bears	Snow White	Cinderella
	The story is about a little girl.	She ate a poisoned apple.	

The teacher should read a general sentence such as, ''The story is about a little girl.'' The children place that sentence under the proper heading. The teacher should have the sentences written on the board to help with spelling. After saying several general sentences, the teacher should give a specific one such as, ''She ate a poisoned apple.'' A discussion should follow discussing which sentences are more specific and which are more general.

31. FACT OR FICTION (Grades 3-5)

A. Purpose: To distinguish between fact and fiction.

B. Materials: Numerous short stories available for choice (both fiction and non-fiction), 3 x 5 cards and pencils will be needed.

C. Introduction to the Class: Instruct the children to choose a story to read silently. After finishing the story, the children are to fill out a card similar to the following:

Title_________________
Author_________________
Fact or Fiction _______

Now the students are to select a partner. They should trade books and read each other's story. They then should fill out a second card like the one shown. When both students finish, they are to compare their cards.

32. DRAWING CONCLUSIONS (Grades 3-5)

A. Purpose: To learn to make predictions and to draw sensible conclusions.

B. Materials: A short story which is unfamiliar to every child, paper and pencils will be needed.

C. Introduction to the Class: Read a short story to the class. Stop when the students seem to be well-involved in the plot. The children are instructed to answer a set of questions similar to the following: (These will vary depending on the content of the story used.)

1. Who do you think will win the race?

2. How long do you think it took the main character to finish?

3. How can you tell that the mother liked her job?

4. What do you think happened when the main character got home?

5. Do you think the main character was happpy or sad?

6. Why did the main character do her shopping before taking care of her house?

7. How old do you think the main character is?

8. During what time of day did the story take place?

The teacher should make sure that the answers to the questions she asks are not specifically stated in the story read.

33. CAUSE AND EFFECT (Grades 3-5)

A. Purpose: To teach students to pick out the cause of an event as well as the effects of that cause.

B. Materials: Provide paper, pencils and any short story or picture book.

C. Introduction to the Class: Read a short story to the class. Next, instruct the students to divide their papers into two columns. At the top of the first column, they should write ''Cause'', and at the top of the second column, ''Effect''. Make a list of events which happened in the story under the heading ''Cause''. After listing what happened, go through each event and discuss what happened after this event because the incident occurred. After completing this, use another story to reverse the lesson, listing the effects first and then the causes. Have the students repeat the procedure independently picking a book of his or her choice.

CAUSE	EFFECT

34. MAKING INFERENCES (Grades 2-5)

A. Purpose: To teach children to make educated guesses based on a limited number of facts.

B. Materials: A picture book with very large pictures will be needed.

C. Introduction to the Class: Select a picture book with large pictures and a number of characters. Hold the picture for the class to see. For the purpose of an example, use the book, <u>Little Black Goes to the Circus</u> by Walter Farley. ''In this picture are many things. You see Mr. Bruno with a top hat standing in front of a big tent. Beside him sits a monkey on a tricycle and a little boy sitting on Little Black, his pony. What can you tell me about this story just by looking at this picture?''

35. SCANNING FOR RHYMING WORDS (Grades 3-5)

A. Purpose: To teach students to scan a selection to locate an answer.

B. Materials: A series of books on poetry, enough for one for each student, paper and pencils will be needed.

C. Introduction to the Class: Tell the children they have five minutes to write down as many rhyming words as they can. The child with the most words wins the game.

D. Variation: When the above game is completed, have two students trade lists of rhyming words. They are then to write a two line poem using the rhyming words on the list. For example:

Poem: ''Firefly'' by Elizabeth Madox Roberts

> A little light is going by,
> Is going up to see the sky,
> A little light with wings.
>
> I never could have thought of it,
> To have a little bug all lit,
> And made to go on wings.

Rhyming words chosen:

> by, sky, it, lit

Example two line poem:

> The stars in the sky
> Seemed to float on by.

36. ALPHABET RACE (Grades K-4)

A. Purpose: To teach students how to skim through books.

B. Materials: Pencils, paper and a selection of picture books, enough for one per student, will be needed.

C. Introduction to the Class: The students are to letter their papers a through z down the left side of their papers. When the teacher says ''go'', they are to open their books and find a word with the letter ''a'' in it, then ''b'' and proceed through ''z''. They are to write these words on their papers next to the corresponding letter. The first person to write all the words through the letter ''z'' wins the game. The winner of the game could also be determined by setting a time limit.

37. DRAW A CREATURE (Grades 1-4)

A. Purpose: To motivate students to use their imagination.

B. Materials: Provide a duplicated sheet for each child

with a figure of a triangle, a square, or a circle on it, pencils and paper.

C. Introduction to the Class: Read the story, <u>Where the Wild Things Are</u>, by Maurice Sendak. Explain to the children that they are going to draw a wild thing, beginning with the shape on their duplicated sheet. The teacher should draw an example of a creature on the chalkboard. The beginning of the creature should be one of the figures on the duplicated sheet.

Example:

The teacher will use the language experience technique to get the children to tell him/her what to write. Leave the story and the picture on the board while the children work on this activity. The teacher should give each student a paper with a large triangle, square or circle on it. They are instructed to make something out of their shape and write a story about it. These stories can be shared with the class.

38. SOUNDS (Grades 1-5)

A. Purpose: To enhance comprehension.

B. Materials: Provide a selection of picture books, paper and pencils.

C. Introduction to the Class: The teacher should read a picture book to the class and on the chalkboard write the word, "sounds." In class discussion, the children should suggest sounds from the story to write under that heading. For example, from the book Stand Back, Said the Elephant, I'm Going to Sneeze by Patricia Thomas you will find the following:

<u>Sounds</u>

Elephant talking	Fish talking
Buffalo talking	Zebra saying, "Yipes"
Monkey talking	Hippopotamus talking
Bird talking	Mouse's "Boo"
Bees buzzing	Elephant laughing
Fly talking	Elephant crying
Bear talking	Crocodile talking

When the activity is finished, each child is given a picture book to use in repeating this exercise independently.

39. FOLLOWING DIRECTIONS (Grades 2-4)

A. Purpose: To learn to follow directions.

B. Materials: A picture book, a duplicated sheet similar to the one shown and pencils will be needed.

C. Introduction to the Class: The teacher should select a picture book to read to the children. The title of the book serves as a start for the following written exercise:

1. <u>One Kitten for Kim</u>

2. Change each k to m. (One Mitten for Mim)

3. Change the it in Mim to O. (One Mitten for Mom)

4. Leave out the word that rhymes with kitten. (One for Mom)

5. Write only the last word. (Mom)

40. I'M THINKING OF AN ANIMAL (Grades 1-4)

A. Purpose: To practice reasoning and listening comprehension skills.

B. Materials: Two picture books with animals as characters and sentence strips will be needed.

C. Introduction to the Class: The teacher should begin by reading two picture books to the children. These books should have numerous animal characters. The teacher should then write a sentence describing an animal on each sentence strip. Next, read these sentences to the children and the children must guess which animal is being described. Older children could write their own descriptive sentences and read them to the class.

41. PUTTING IDEAS IN ORDER (Grades 2-4)

A. Purpose: To learn story sequencing.

B. Materials: Provide four picture books and sentence strips.

C. Introduction to the Class: The teacher should read the four short picture books to the class. After reading the stories, the class should be divided into four groups. Each group is given a set of sentence strips with sentences dealing with their book printed on them. The group must put the sentences in order and choose a person to read the story to the class. The class decides if the stories make sense in the order they are read.

42. LET'S PLAN A TRIP (Grades 3-5)

A. Purpose: To improve comprehension and business letter writing.

B. Materials: A selection of picutre books or short stories, paper and pencils will be needed.

C. Introduction to the Class: Each child should read a short story or picture book with settings somewhere in the

United States. The teacher then should write a sample business letter on the chalkboard. This letter should request information on a particular location. Each child will write to the Chamber of Commerce of the capital city of the state which is the setting of his/her book. When the brochures come, the children should share them with the class.

43. NAME THAT STORY (Grades 3-5)

A. Purpose: To write appropriate titles for stories.

B. Materials: Provide a selection of picture books, paper and pencils.

C. Introduction to the Class: Put a paper cover on the front of a picture book. Read the book to the children. This book should be unfamiliar to everyone. Each child must write a title for the story. After all the children share their titles, the teacher should take the cover off the book to show the actual title.

44. WHAT KIND OF MARK? (Grades 2-4)

A. Purpose: To use punctuation marks to improve comprehension.

B. Materials: A picture book, three large cards with an exclamation mark, a question mark or a period on them will be needed.

C. Introduction to the Class: The teacher should read some sentences from a picture book to the class changing the intonation of her voice to show excitement or interrogation. Three students are given the punctuation cards. After each sentence is read, the class should decide which mark goes at the end of the sentence. When the activity is completed, the teacher should read the entire story to the children.

45. WHEN, WHERE, WHO? (Grades 2-5)

A. Purpose: To enhance comprehension.

B. Materials: A duplicated sheet similar to that shown, pencils, sentence strips and a picture book will be needed.

Who	When	Where

C. Introduction to the Class: The teacher should write some phrases from a picture book on sentence strips. The picture book is read to the children. The teacher then holds up the sentence strip and the children must copy it under the proper heading.

46. CHORAL READING (Grades 1-5)

A. Purpose: To practice choral reading.

B. Materials: Several picture books will be needed.

C. Introduction to the Class: The children should be divided into groups of four. Two of the children read the first sentence of the story. The other children provide an echo by reading the same sentence again.

47. DESCRIPTIVE WORDS (Grades 3-5)

A. Purpose: To use descriptive words.

B. Materials: Provide three picture books, pencils, a shoe box, paper and strips of paper with one adjective written on each one.

C. Introduction to the Class: The teacher reads the three picture books to the class. Each child draws three words from the box. On their papers, they are to write:

I think _________ is _________ because _________

____

____

The children can put any one of the three story titles in the first space, but the second space should have the adjective drawn from the box.

48. RIDDLE BOX (Grades 3-6)

A. Purpose: To interest students in reading more books.

B. Materials: A large box, paper and pencils will be needed.

C. Introduction to the Class: Cut the top off a large box and decorate similar to the illustration. This box is a question box containing riddles about stories which have been read in class. Any pupil who wants to may put a riddle in the box. The riddle should describe the book, and then ask for the title of the book. The riddle could give the title of the book, describe a character in it and then ask for the character's name. One such riddle might be: "I am a book about a little boy who becomes friends with a dinosaur," or "I rode on a dinosaur's back. Who am I?" The answers should be written on the back of each sheet of paper. Answers: <u>Danny and the Dinosaur</u>; Danny

49. READO (Grades 3-6)

A. Purpose: To review stories read.

B. Materials: Provide a "reado" card for each child. These cards are divided into 16 squares with a book title in each square. Short stories may be used for older children's cards.

C. Introduction to the Class: This game is played like "Bingo." The caller may read the book title, the author or leading characters in the stories. The players match the information given to the title on their cards. A winner is determined by having titles covering the squares horizontally, diagonally or the four corners. All of the book or story titles used must be ones which have been read to or shared with the entire class.

50. KEEPING A LOG (Grades 2-6)

A. Purpose: To provide a picture of student growth.

B. Materials: One notebook per child will be needed.

C. Introduction to the Class: The term "log" is introduced through the explanation of its use by a ship's captain to record events during the day. Each child is to keep his own reading log. In this log, the student should be instructed to record any or all of the following:

1. The title and author of the book read.

2. Interesting new words and their definitions.

3. Written answers to questions given by the teacher.

4. Reactions to the stories.

5. Lists of word groups, such as synonyms, antonyms or homonyms found in the story.

6. Creative writing of prose or poetry dealing with the subject of the story.

51. VISUAL BOOK REPORTS (Grades 3-6)

A. Purpose: To write book reports using visual aids.

B. Materials: Provide magazines, scissors, felt pens, paste, poster board and index cards.

C. Introduction to the Class: The children should be instructed to select a book to be read for a book report. The students are to cut pictures from magazines or newspapers that depict an idea, theme or actual scene from the book they have read. The pictures are to be glued to poster board, leaving a large border around them. On this border, the students are to arrange words or phrases that explain or describe the story. They are instructed to look for vivid adjectives or verbs. On the lower back corner of the poster board, they are to attach an index card. The index card should include a brief summary of the book's plot, the author and the publisher. Book reports using visual techniques help the students to grasp the meaning of a story very effectively.

52. LET'S HAVE AN INTERVIEW (Grades 4-6)

A. Purpose: To pratice interviewing skills.

B. Materials: Numerous books should be available to allow for choice.

C. Introduction to the Class: Two students read the same book and work as partners in this activity. One student takes the part of the author of the book and the other student takes the part of the interviewer. The topic of the interview could be anything. For example, the author could state how he/she happened to write the book or how he/she felt about one of the characters. Other students may choose to do dialogues between the author and one of the characters or between two characters. The teacher serves as a guide giving ideas for questions. Have some of the interviews presented to the class.

53. STUDY SKILLS (Grades 3-5)

A. Purpose: To aid in the development of study skills.

B. Materials: A selection of picture books, 3 x 5 cards with directions printed on them, paper and pencils will be needed.

C. Introduction to the Class: The teacher should prepare eight or ten cards by printing some directions on them. They should be prepared following some of these examples:

Find five compound words in the picture books in the room.

Find five words with more than two syllables.

Find five words with a prefix or a suffix.

Find five contractions or their corresponding word pairs.

Find five words which end in ''st''.

54. FIGURATIVE SPEECH (Grades 4-5)

A. Purpose: To learn to recognize types of figurative language.

B. Materials: Choose a short story to read.

C. Introduction to the Class: Read the short story to the class. Discuss the meaning of the terms simile, metaphor and personification in class discussion. Next, go through the story, paragraph by paragraph, picking out the similes, metaphors and personification in the selection. Write them on the chalkboard under the proper heading.

Simile	Metaphor	Personification
as brave as a lion	a heart of stone	The trees trembled in the wind

simile - a figure of speech in which two dissimilar things are compared by the use of like or as.

metaphor - a figure of speech in which a word denoting one object is used in place of another to suggest a likeness between them.

personification - a figure of speech in which a lifeless thing or quality is spoken of as if alive.

55. RIDDLES (Grades 2-5)

A. Purpose: To enhance comprehension.

B. Materials: Several books dealing with riddles, paper and pencils will be needed.

C. Introduction to the Class: The teacher should read some "What am I?" riddles to the class. Divide the class into groups of four or five. Each group is to come up with some riddles to stump the class. The younger children will probably need to use the riddle books, while the older ones will write some of their own.

56. BOOK AUCTION (Grades 3-4)

A. Purpose: To motivate extra reading by holding an auction.

B. Materials: A number of books will be needed. You will also need ten markers similar to those used in Bingo games for each student.

C. Introduction to the Class: The teacher should start by saying, "Here's a book you'll enjoy, Where the Wild Things Are. It has a lot of illustrations and is very exciting. Who will bid one marker? I have one. Who will bid two?" The bidding continues until it reaches ten markers. The student bidding the highest gets to read the book. Remind the students that they only have ten markers and they should bid carefully. Each child is expected to bid and read one book. The auction concept could be spread over a number of weeks with the special books checked out only on an auction basis.

57. ADVERTISE YOUR BOOK (Grades 1-6)

A. Purpose: To motivate extra reading.

B. Materials: Provide poster board cut into 8 x 10 squares, popsicle sticks, white glue and paint or crayons.

C. Introduction to the Class: Distribute four popsicle sticks and one board to each student. Instuct them to make miniature billboards advertising their books by gluing the sticks together to form a stand and drawing or writing on the poster. Make certain the students have decided what feature will be advertised to make others interested in the book before they actually start on the poster. This will prevent the posters from being cluttered with so many ideas that it's difficult to decipher the meaning. Display the completed billboards on a bulletin board.

58. MAKE AN OUTLINE (Grades 3-8)

A. Purpose: To get students to use the table of contents in a book to get a quick idea of what the book is about. Also, to give practice in making an outline.

B. Materials: A selection of fiction books, each containing a table of contents, pencils and paper will be needed.

C. Introduction to the Class: The basic outline form should be written on the chalkboard. The book is divided into three major parts. The A, B and C shown in the example should be the major happenings in each chapter.

   I. Introduction to the story
      A.
      B.
      C.

  II. Major Action or Problem
      A.
      B.
      C.

III. Solution
   A.
   B.
   C.

59. WHAT'S MY LINE? (Grades 2-5)

A. Purpose: To arouse students' interest in various books.

B. Materials: Several copies of five different library books will be needed.

C. Introduction to the Class: At the beginning of the week, the teacher gives a short introduction of the books to arouse interest. The children are instructed to read each of the books before Friday. The topics of the books should be similar. (For example, all about outer space adventures.) On Friday, after everyone has had a chance to read the books, pick five students from the class to play "What's My Line?" One of the five students is chosen to be "it" and selects a character from one of the books to portray. The panel can ask only "yes" and "no" questions to determine who the person is portraying and what book he/she is from. Each panel member asks one question at a time and the panel has ten guesses to determine the character. Give others a chance to play the game.

60. TIC-TAC-TOE (Grades 3-6)

A. Purpose: To create interest in reading library books.

B. Materials: Provide a tic-tac-toe game board such as the following:

Little Don Pedro	Nothing At All	Fly High, Fly Low
Listen, Rabbit	Petunia	Surprise Egg
May I Bring A Friend?	Sam and the Firefly	Thin Ice

C. Introduction to the Class: Each child should have read all nine of the stories on the tic-tac-toe game board before attempting to play the game. The class writes questions about each story on slips of paper. The papers are put into an envelope, using one envelope for each story. Two children play the game.

The players draw a question from the envelope of the story of their choice. If answered correctly, the player puts either an x or an o over the appropriate square. The game continues until the x, the o or the cat wins.

61. MOBILES (Grades K-6)

A. Purpose: To expand a favorite story.

B. Materials: Magazines, construction paper, newspaper, two sticks for each child and thread will be needed.

C. Introduction to the Class: Each child will make a mobile depicting the story he has read. He or she is to hang pictures, words or anything that reminds him or her of that story. The students may want to attach the title of the story with the other pictures and things.

Tie the two sticks together where they cross. Thread the string through the top of the objects being used and attach the other end of the strings to the sticks. Attach another string to the sticks so that they can be hung from the ceiling.

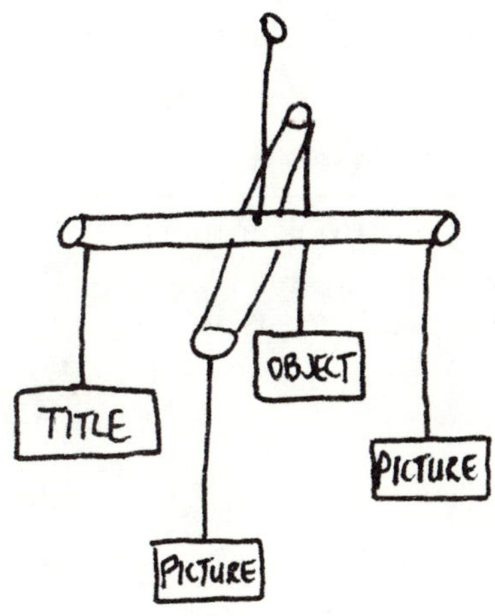

62. WRITE A TABLE OF CONTENTS (Grades 3-8)

A. Purpose: To provide practice in determining the main idea.

B. Materials: A selection of novels with no table of contents or chapter titles, paper and pencils will be needed.

C. Introduction to the Class: The students are to read a novel and make a table of contents for their novel. This is done by deciding the main idea and action in the chapters and giving each chapter a title.

63. STANDARD BOOK REPORT FORM (Grades 3-8)

A. Purpose: To provide a form for students to follow which can be used with any book.

B. Materials: A selection of books at varying reading levels, paper and pencils will be needed.

C. Introduction to the Class: Prepare a form such as the following:

Book Report

1. The name of the book is _______________________

2. The author of the book is_______________________

3. The book tells about_______________________
____

4. The part I like best is _______________________
____

The students are instructed to draw a picture about the story at the top of the page. The open-ended sentences should appear on the bottom of the form. After reading a number of books, each student can make a book of his/her reports to take home.

64. DOING WORDS (Grades 2-5)

A. Purpose: To recognize verbs in a selection.

B. Materials: A selection of picture books, paper and pencils will be needed.

C. Introduction to the Class: Each child is given a picture book. They read their books, writing down all of the doing words they see. They select a partner, trade books with him/her and do the same exercise again. The two will then compare their lists.

65. MIXED UP SENTENCES (Grades 2-4)

A. Purpose: To construct sentences using a given set of words.

B. Materials: A selection of picture books, paper and pencils will be needed.

C. Introduction to the Class: Each child should be given a picture book, and a set of ten strips of paper. They are instructed to find a sentence with ten or less words and write one word on each strip of paper.

They choose a partner and trade papers. Each student must arrange his partner's words to form a sentence and then read it to the class.

66. NEW VOCABULARY IN INDEPENDENT READINGS (Grades 3- 8)

A. Purpose: To increase each student's vocabulary.

B. Materials: Provide library books, paper and pencils.

C. Introduction to the Class: Each student will keep a record of the new words encountered as he/she reads. This information will be shared with the class.

Date	Book Title	Author	New Word	Complete Sen. from the story	Def.

67. LET'S PLAY BASEBALL (Grades 3-5)

A. Purpose: To enhance comprehension.

B. Materials: Provide numerous picture books for students to read.

C. Introduction to the Class: Prior to playing this game, numerous picture books or short stories should be read to the class. Four chairs are placed in the room to resemble a baseball diamond.

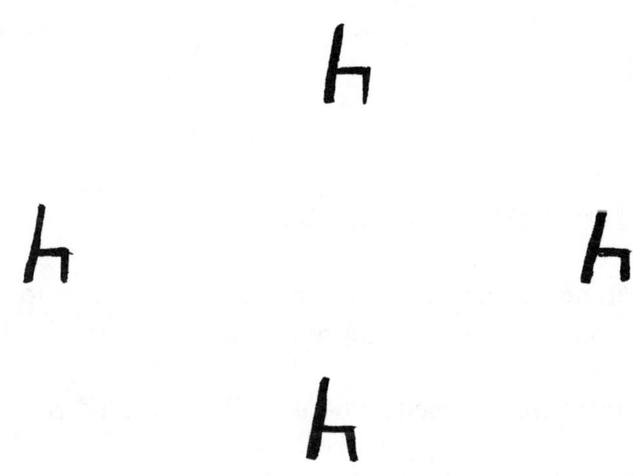

Two teams should be chosen. The teacher makes a statement dealing with the plot, characters or setting of a story. The player must name the story to which the teacher has referred. Runs are tallied, as in baseball, and three wrong answers make three outs.

68. NONFICTION BOOKS (Grades 3-8)

A. Purpose: To give students opportunities to read nonfiction.

B. Materials: A selection of nonfiction, informational books, poster board, pencils and markers will be needed.

C. Introduction to the Class: Students are instructed to read their informative book and make a poster listing six facts learned from each book. The posters can be displayed around the room. Each student is asked to share the poster orally with the group, giving the author, title, the main idea the author wanted to get across and discussing the six facts learned.

69. INTONATION (Grades 2-5)

A. Purpose: To teach children to use their voices to show feeling and to enhance comprehension.

B. Materials: A picture book will be needed.

C. Introduction to the Class: The teacher reads a picture book to the class. After finishing the book, the teacher selects some sentences to reread. One student repeats the sentence the teacher read using the same intonation and tone the teacher used. Care should be taken in the selection of sentences to include exclamations, commands and questions.

70. MAKE MEANINGFUL SENTENCES (Grades 2-5)

A. Purpose: To recognize meaningful sentences.

B. Materials: Provide a picture book, paper and pencils.

C. Introduction to the Class: The teacher should read

a picture book to the class and copy some sentences out of the story on strips of paper. On other strips, write the same sentences with the words in the wrong order.

Example:

The giant was asleep at the table.

Table at giant the asleep was the

Divide the class into groups of five children. Give each group ten correct sentences along with their corresponding mixed up sentences. They are to match the correct sentence with the incorrect one. Each student will read a meaningful sentence to the class.

71. LET'S CLASSIFY (Grades 3-6)

A. Purpose: To learn how to classify books.

B. Materials: Provide fifty 3 x 5 cards of one color, six 3 x 5 cards of another color, a marking pen and poster board for constructing game boards.

C. Introduction to the Class: Each student should construct a board which contains 12 pockets. Print the title of a book on each of the fifty cards of one color. On the six cards of another color, print these categories: Science, Biography, Humor or Fairy Tales, Sports, Science Fiction and Myths or Legends.

The title cards are shuffled and dealt to each player until all of the pockets of everyone's board is filled. The students

take turns drawing a category card. They then remove from
the pockets those titles of books which belong in that
category. He replaces the category card to the bottom of the
pile. (Example: If a child draws the category card
''Biography', he may remove all stories about the lives of
people.) The game ends when one player removes all his/her
cards.

72. COLOR WORDS (Grades K-4)

A. Purpose: To recognize color words and to categorize
objects.

B. Materials: A selection of picture books, pencils and
a prepared duplicated sheet similar to the following will be
needed.

Red	Green	Yellow	Blue	Orange	Black	White

C. Introduction to the Class: Each child is given a picture book and a copy of the duplicated sheet. The children
are to read their books and place the objects in the story under
the appropriate describing color.

73. WHAT SEASON IS IT? (Grades 2-4)

A. Purpose: To categorize through reading comprehension.

B. Materials: A selection of picture books will be needed.

C. Introduction to the Class: The teacher should write the following headings on the chalkboard:

Autumn	Winter	Spring	Summer

Each child reads a picture book and places the title of the story under the season in which the story takes place. When everyone is through, the children should share something about their books, telling why they believe the story took place in that season.

74. LET'S CATEGORIZE (Grades 3-5)

A. Purpose: To learn to classify.

B. Materials: Provide a selection of nonfiction books dealing with a main topic (example: foods), paper and pencils.

C. Introduction to the Class: Two students will work together in this activity. They are given one book and are instructed to find words to place under the proper heading. Using books dealing with food, the following categories might be used:

1. Cereal and Breads

2. Meats

3. Vegetables and Fruits

4. Milk group

The categories can be changed to fit information on any topic.

75. CATEGORIES (Grades 2-4)

A. Purpose: To teach children to categorize.

B. Materials: Paper, pencils and numerous picture books for choice will be needed.

C. Introduction to the Class: Discuss groups of things with the class. Use a sample category to make a list on the chalkboard (for example: foods) Read a picture book to the students. Divide a section of the chalkboard into three pieces. Write the following headings at the top of the board:

People	Places	Things

As a group, complete the list on the chalkboard. Give each student a picture book to read and have him do the above exercise independently. The categories can be changed to fit the books used.

UNIT III
DICTIONARY AND REFERENCE SKILLS

1. WHAT KIND OF BOOK DO YOU LIKE?
(Grades 2-5)

   A. Purpose: To learn to read a table.

   B. Materials: Provide a picture book dealing with sports, a picture book dealing with animals, a fairy tale and a science story. (These subjects can be changed to fit the needs of the group.)

   C. Introduction to the Class: The teacher draws the following table on the chalkboard.

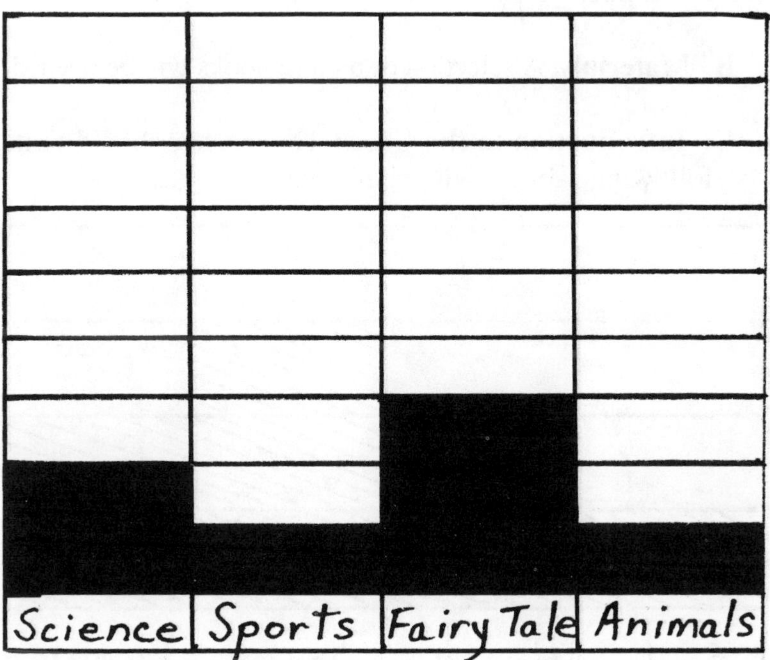

The teacher now reads a short story on each of the topics used. The children are to color a box above the book they liked best. When the table is completed, have the following questions answered in class discussion.

1. How many children are in the class?

2. Which kind of book was liked the most?

3. Which kind of book was liked the least?

2. READING A TABLE (Grades 3-5)

A. Purpose: To gain information from a table.

B. Materials: A selection of picture books will be needed.

C. Introduction to the Class: The teacher should write the following table on the chalkboard.

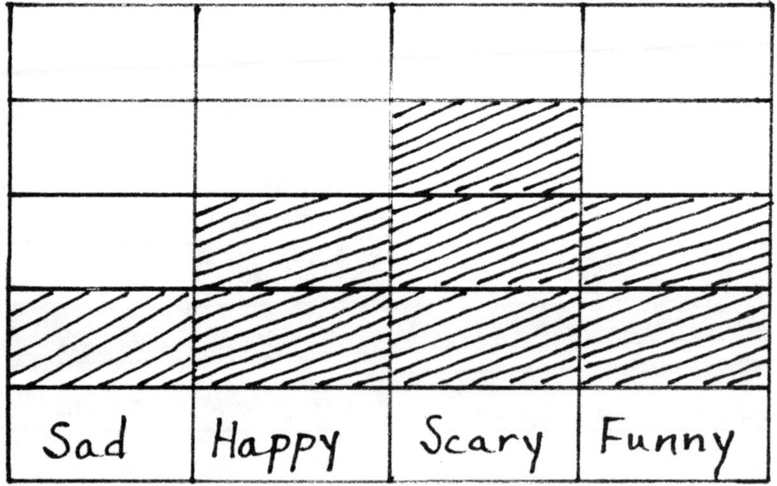

The children are to read a picture book, decide whether it is sad, happy, scary or funny and color in one box over the appropriate word. When this is completed, the group should answer the following questions.

1. How many books were read in all?

2. Which kind of book was read the most?

3. Which kind of book was read the least?

3. ALPHABETICAL ORDER (Grades 3-5)

A. Purpose: To teach alphabetical order.

B. Materials: A selection of picture books, one per child, will be needed.

C. Introduction to the Class: The teacher divides the class into four groups. Every student gets a book. Each group must line its books against the wall in alphabetical order. When the books are all lined against the wall, the groups will change places, serving as a check of their classmates' work.

4. ABC Foods (Grades 2-4)

A. Purpose: To develop vocabulary and teach alphabetical order.

B. Materials: A selection of nonfiction books dealing with kinds of foods, paper and pencils will be needed.

C. Introduction to the Class: The teacher divides the class into five groups. The children are to look in their books for the names of foods and write one for each letter of the alphabet.

Example:

A - Apple

B - Bread

C - Carrots

D - Dessert

5. GUIDE WORDS (Grades 3-5)

A. Purpose: To teach dictionary skills.

B. Materials: A selection of picture books, paper and pencils will be needed.

C. Introduction to the Class: Each child is given a picture book and is instructed to find five words beginning with b, c or d and write them on his paper. The teacher discusses dictionary guide words and explains that we are going to place the words on a pretend dictionary page. The teacher should make the sample dictionary pages on the chalkboard like the example shown.

Bad Bell	Bet Bun	Cat Cent	Cell Cup	Dad Den	Dim Dry

He/she should read and spell the words one at a time and
have the class decide on which page to put each one.

6. LOOK IT UP (Grades 3-5)

A. Purpose: To locate information in encyclopedias and
other reference books.

B. Materials: Picture books, encyclopedias and nonfiction books relating to a particular geographic area will be
needed.

C. Introduction to the Class: Read a picture book or short
story to the class. Talk about where the story takes place.
Choose a book which has a setting in a different geographic
area than your location. Divide the class into six groups. Give
each a topic to study which deals with the location in question. The topics could be as follows:

1. The weather in the area

2. The kind of land in the area

3. The population and kinds of people

4. Places to visit

5. Industry

6. History

The topics could be changed to fit any area.
Have the students share the information they have found with the class.

7. USING THE INDEX (Grades 3-5)

A. Purpose: To teach children to use an index to get information.

B. Materials: Provide paper, pencils and a selection of nonfiction books dealing with a large variety of things in one class. For example, a book about animals would contain an index with the names of all different animals and where to locate information in the book.

C. Introduction to the Class: Each student is given a book like the one described. All of the books should be about the same thing, such as animals. Give the students a list of questions to answer. (The questions should deal with the page on which you would find information on specific animals.)

8. TABLE OF CONTENTS (Grades 2-5)

A. Purpose: To gain information from the table of contents.

B. Materials: A selection of library books with tables of contents in them, paper and pencils will be needed.

C. Introduction to the Class: Each child chooses a partner and is given a book. His/her job is to prepare a set of questions for his/her partner to answer. The teacher should write a sample set of questions on the chalkboard as well as a make believe table of contents. Example:

Table of contents	Questions
Tracey's Cat............7	1. On what pages would you find a mystery?
I Wonder Why?........17	2. On what pages would you find something about animals?
The Mystery...........25	3. On what pages would you find something about a little boy?
What Happened?.......35	4. On what pages would you find somebody asking questions?
The Alligator.........47	

9. USING THE CARD CATALOGUE (Grades 3-5)

A. Purpose: To learn to use the card catalogue.

B. Materials: Provide index cards, pencils, a file box and a selection of picture books.

C. Introduction to the Class: The teacher writes a sample card from a card catalogue on the chalkboard. Example:

```
       F
Bur    Burch, Robert
       Renfroe's Christmas  New York,
       Viking, 1968
       59 p.  illlus.

                    O
```

The teacher should discuss the meaning of the ''F'' and the abbreviations for page and illustrated. Each child should be given a book and should be instructed to make a card to go in our room card catalogue. When each child finishes, he/she puts his/her card in the file box, making sure the cards are in alphabetical order. The ABC order is checked by each student as he places his card in the card catalogue.

UNIT IV
CRITICAL THINKING

1. "BE THE TEACHER" (Grades 3-8)

A. Purpose: To enhance reading comprehension.

B. Materials: Short story collection books, pencils and paper will be needed.

C. Introduction to the Class: Four students are instructed to read the same short story. After reading the story, the students arc asked to write five questions beginning with who, what, where, when, why or how. The student is to record the page number where the answer to the question is found. After this is done, the four students ask each other their questions. If no one can answer a question, the questioner says, "Read page . . . to find the answer to the question." This is done until everyone's questions have been answered in group discussion.

2. WRITING QUESTIONS (Grades 3-8)

A. Purpose: To provide students with practice in developing and answering questions.

B. Materials: Paper, pencils and 4-6 copies of the same book will be needed.

C. Introduction to the Class: A group of 4-6 students each read the same book. Each student is directed to write 6 questions. One question should ask who, one what, one why, one when, one where and one how. These questions are given to a student outside their group. The readers form a panel and must answer the questions given to them. The writer of the questions is asked to answer his own question.

3. FOLLOWING DIRECTIONS (Grades 3-8)

A. Purpose: To give students practice in following written directions.

B. Materials: A selection of "How to do it" books and a variety of art materials will be needed.

C. Introduction to the Class: The students are instructed to read a "How to do it" book and select something from it to demonstrate to the class. Craft books are especially good in that the demonstrations are short and show a finished product. If a book is selected which deals with making a long term project, the student should demonstrate only a step in the process.

4. ANIMAL BOOKS (Grades 3-8)

A. Purpose: To interrelate science concepts with reading by showing animals and their habitats.

B. Materials: Books about animals and cardboard boxes will be needed.

C. Introduction to the Class: The students are to select a book about some kind of animal. Each book can be either fiction or nonfiction. They are instructed to make a diorama showing the animal in its natural habitat. A cardboard box can be used for the stage. The students can use any materials to show the animal and its surroundings. The students should be encouraged to use real materials, such as grass from the outdoors, to make their scene seem real.

5. SCIENCE FICTION (Grades 3-8)

A. Purpose: To provide practice in distinguishing between realism and fantasy.

B. Materials: A set of science fiction stories, paper and pencils will be needed.

C. Introduction to the Class: The students are instructed to read a science fiction story. Afterwards, the students discuss their stories deciding which parts of it could be true and which could not. Students will notice that there is more that could possibly be true in older science fiction stories because of the advancement in space travel and technology.

6. "TIME LINE" (Grades 3-8)

A. Purpose: To give students experience in using time lines.

B. Materials: A selection of books relating to American History, paper and pencils will be needed.

C. Introduction to the Class: Each student is instructed to draw his/her own time line showing the major events in his/her life. An example can be done on the board.

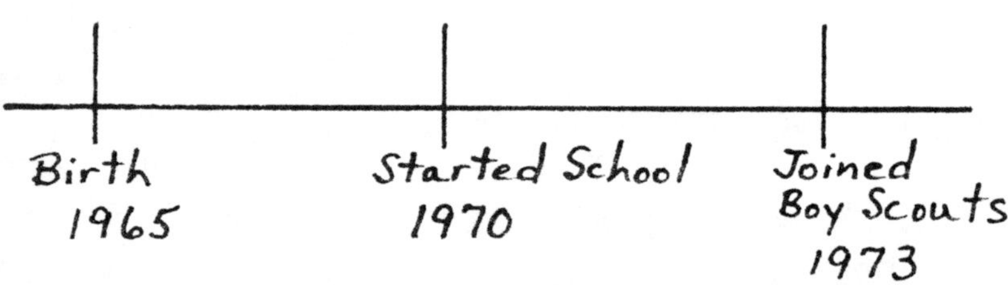

The teacher must select a number of books all relating to American History. These can be fiction or nonfiction. The students must decide where their story should appear on the U.S. History time line which should be displayed across the front board. (It is important that the books selected cover the span of U.S. History from the very beginning to the present day.)

7. BIOGRAPHY (Grades 3-8)

A. Purpose: To teach the term ''biography'' and to provide students with opportunities to experience a part of some important person's life.

B. Materials: A selection of biographies, costume clothes, 3 x 5 cards and pencils will be needed.

C. Introduction to the Class: The students are instructed to select a biography. They are to read the biography with the specific purpose of getting a good picture of the person. They are to dress up like and pretend to be that person while telling the class the story of "his" or "her" life. Each student is given a 3 x 5 card. On it he/she is to write the name of his/her book, the author, when and where the person lived and why he/she is remembered. These cards can be displayed on a biography bulletin board.

8. WHO, WHAT, WHERE, WHEN, HOW, WHY? (Grades 3-8)

A. Purpose: To provide students with practice in reading with specific question words in mind.

B. Materials: Provide library books, paper and pencils.

C. Introduction to the Class: The students are to divide the front and back of their paper into three sections each, as pictured in the example. They are instructed to copy sentences from their book; underlining the phrase which answers the question.

Front

Who	What	Where
<u>Danny</u> looked out of the window.	<u>Snow</u> had covered the ground.	Carol ran <u>around the corner.</u>

<u>Back</u>

When	How	Why
The <u>next day</u> we planned to leave.	Elizabeth ran <u>quickly</u> home.	Elizabeth ran quickly home <u>because she was scared.</u>

9. SHOWING EMOTIONS (Grades 3-8)

A. Purpose: To provide experiences for students to perceive how an author uses vocabulary to describe feelings.

B. Materials: Provide library books, paper and pencils.

C. Introduction to the Class: The teacher should write some feeling words on the board such as the following:

angry	sad	worried
excited	lonely	shy
happy	embarrassed	
delighted	disgusted	

The students are instructed to find a set number of sentences or phrases in their story that the author has used to describe feelings. THe students should divide their paper as follows:

Sentence Used	Feeling
"I can't stand this anymore!"	anger

A. Purpose: To provide the students with practice in using the context to figure out the meaning of an unfamiliar word.

B. Materials: Library books, paper, pencils, 3 x 5 cards and dictionaries will be needed.

C. Introduction to the Class: The students are directed to find five sentences in their books which contain an unfamiliar word. They are to copy each sentence on a 3 x 5 card, leaving out the unfamiliar word. The unfamiliar word and its definition are written on the back of the same card. Instead of writing the unfamiliar word, the students are directed to insert the word BEEP. The student reads his sentence to the class using the word BEEP in place of the unfamiliar word. The class must determine the meaning of BEEP in the sentence. When this is done, the unfamiliar word and dictionary definition is shared with the class. The class might want to keep a record of these unfamiliar words.

11. BUILDING VOCABULARY (Grades 3-8)

A. Purpose: To encourage the student to use a variety of words.

B. Materials: Library books about people, paper and pencils will be needed.

C. Introduction to the Class: The teacher should write the following directions on the chalkboard or provide a duplicated sheet.

---

1) Find 10 words in your book which describe how a person might feel.

2) Find 10 words in your book which describe how a person might look.

3) Find 10 words in your book which could be used to describe a place.

4) Find 10 words in your book which are doing words or verbs which show action.

---

12. LISTENING FOR ACTION (Grades 3-8)

A. Purpose: To enhance listening skills.

B. Materials: Provide a short story to read to the class, paper and pencils.

C. Introduction to the Class: The teacher tells the students to listen for the action words in a particular passage. When the passage is read, the students are to write down the verbs in order and write as many as they can remember. Have the students keep a record of their own progress. The length and difficulty of the passage can be increased as improvement is seen. It is important to begin with only a paragraph of the short story at a time. This is difficult and could get frustrating.

13. ACT IT OUT (Grades 3-8)

A. Purpose: Book sharing.

B. Materials: A selection of story titles will be needed.

C. Introduction to the Class: The students take turns playing charades with the rest of the class. They are to act out each word of the book title.

12 WIDELY USED CHARADE SYMBOLS

1. Book. Hands open, together

2. Play. Move Hands from center.

3. Movie. Hold camera left; crank by right ear.

4. "Song," or "Musical," when combined with movie or play.

5. Words in Title. Hold up number of fingers.

6. Number of Syllables. Tap number of divisions on forearm.

7. Longer Word. Move open hands outward.

8. Shorter Word. Move open hands inward.

9. Little Word. Thumb and forefinger

10. Article-- "THE".

11. Whole Thing. Move hands outward overhead.

12. Sounds Like. Stroke ear with forefinger.

14. PANEL DISCUSSION (Grades 3-8)

A. Purpose: To stimulate critical thinking and to provide experiences in working on a group project.

B. Materials: Provide sets of books by the same author, paper and pencils.

C. Introduction to the Class: Four or five people should read a different book by the same author. They then should plan a panel discussion and each student shares his/her story with the class. Then, the panel discusses such questions as how the books are alike or different. The group members should also tell if they would like to read more books by the same author.

15. LET'S BE SAFE (Grades 3-8)

A. Purpose: To instruct students in safety.

B. Materials: A selection of books on safety, poster board or white construction paper, markers, crayons and colored pens will be needed.

C. Introduction to the Class: Each student is to read a nonfiction book on safety. It can be on bicycle safety, pedestrian safety or bus safety. It can also deal with being careful with such things as electricity, fire or poisons. The students are to make a poster about their book. On the poster should be the title and author of the book and an illustration about the book's content.

16. DEMONSTRATE AN EXPERIMENT (Grades 3-8)

A. Purpose: To interest students in the sciences and to encourage critical thinking.

B. Materials: A series of books with sample science experiments will be needed.

C. Introduction to the Class: Each student is to find an experiment to demonstrate to the class. Several students can use the same book. The experiments chosen must require readily available materials, either from outdoors or inside. Before demonstrating the experiment, the student must write a report on the experiment so it can be reviewed by the teacher.

CIRCUITS — OPENED AND CLOSED

CLOSED

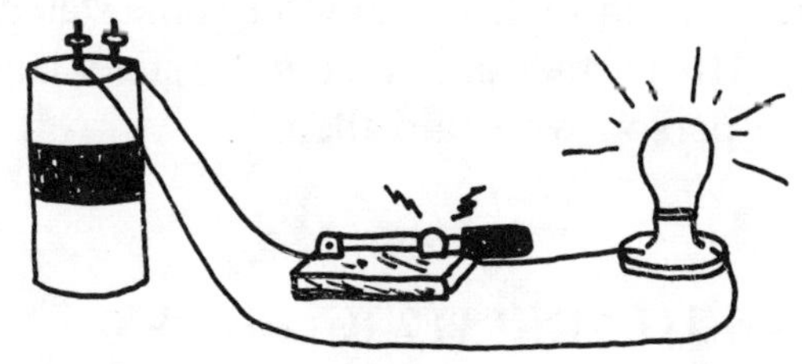

OPENED

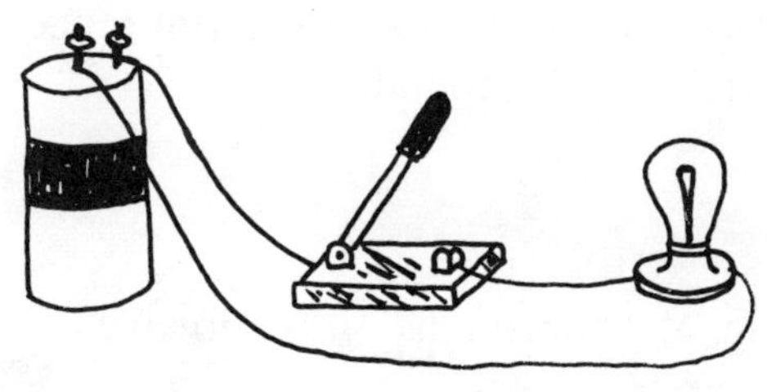

17. MATCH THE STATEMENT (Grades 3-8)

A. Purpose: To enhance inferential comprehension.

B. Materials: A selection of books, paper and pencils will be needed.

C. Introduction to the Class: Two students must read the same story. Each student is to write some statements made in the story. His partner is to match the statements with the name of the person who said them.

18. WHERE TO FIND IT? (Grades 3-8)

A. Purpose: To make students aware of the types of reference books that are available to them.

B. Materials: Provide a set of encyclopedias, dictionaries, an atlas and an almanac.

C. Introduction to the Class: The students are given a list of phrases and must choose the reference book where the information can be found.

Example:

1. Spelling of "thorough" - Dictionary

2. Boundaries of Mexico - Atlas

3. Information on a past president - Encyclopedia

4. Weather predictions - Almanac

19. COMPARE TWO BOOKS (Grades 3-8)

A. Purpose: To provide practice in critical thinking.

B. Materials: Sets of books by the same author, a duplicated sheet, paper and pencils will be needed.

C. Introduction to the Class: The students are to read two books by the same author. They are to compare the two books. The students can be given some ideas to start depending on the grade level involved.

1. Fiction or nonfiction?

2. Purpose to inform or entertain?

3. Setting?

4. Types of characters?

5. Happy or sad?

20. OBSERVATION TIME (Grades 5-8)

A. Purpose: To enhance critical thinking and to teach students to be alert observers.

B. Materials: A selection of picture books, paper and pencils will be needed.

C. Introduction to the Class: Each student is to select a short picture book to read to a primary class. Each student has a partner. The partner is instructed to sit in front with the reader and take notes on the behavior of the listeners. The partner writes a report of his observation. Based on the listener's behavior, the observer must decide if the book was good for a group of children the age of those involved.

21. HAVE A CONFERENCE (Grades 3-8)

A. Purpose: To provide one-to-one interaction between student and teacher. The teacher is able to know each student better and can see the level of difficulty of the material the student is reading.

B. Materials: Books, paper and pencils will be needed.

C. Introduction to the Class: The students are given a list of questions to respond to as they read their book. They write down the answers and then hold a conference with the teacher to discuss them.

Examples follow:

1. What is the most exciting part of your book?

2. Make a list of words you did not know.

3. Who is the most interesting character?

4. Tell me something about the author.

5. Can you think of anyone who is like a character in your book?

22. MY READING RECORD (Grades 3-8)

A. Purpose: To have students keep a record of the books they read.

B. Materials: Provide library books, paper, pencils and a form such as the following:

Date	Title of Book	Author	F or NF	Plot	Like

C. Introduction to the Class: The students should each have a form on which to keep track of the books he or she has read. At the end of a designated time, the students will play the part of a news reporter and share this information with their classmates.

UNIT V
CREATIVE WRITING

1. WRITING PLAYS (Grades 3-8)

A. Purpose: To provide practice in creative writing and to make students aware of the major components of a play (character, time, setting, sound effects, stage directions, cues, etc.).

B. Materials: Provide a selection of short, high action novels, paper, art media, pencils and cardboard.

C. Introduction to the Class: The teacher selects a variety of high action novels and suggests that two or three students work together. Each person in the group must read the novel. The group is instructed to rewrite the novel in a play form. They are instructed to:

(l) Divide the actions into three acts. Each act would be in one location so that a stage backdrop could be made.

(2) Decrease the number of major characters to three, if necessary.

(3) Develop the characters through conversation.

(4) Write stage directions wherever needed (a door slamming etc.).

(5) Read the play to the class.

2. MYSTERY (Grades 3-8)

A. Purpose: To give students opportunities in creative writing.

B. Materials: Mystery books, paper and pencils will be needed.

C. Introduction to the Class: Each student is instructed to read a mystery book and write a summary of the main plot. The summary should include all of the main characters and the part they play in unraveling the mystery at hand. The summary should not reveal the ending of the story. The students trade summaries and write the ending to their partner's book. After this is done the partners discuss the true ending of their stories.

3. CHARACTERIZATION (Grades 3-8)

A. Purpose: To provide practice in creative writing.

B. Materials: A selection of novels, paper and pencils will be needed.

C. Introduction to the Class: The students are instructed to read a novel thinking about the personality of a main character. They are to make a list of adjectives they feel describe the main character. Then, they are to write a new adventure for the main charaacter, pretending that three years have passed. They are to plan events in their story which depict the same characteristics of the main character in their original book.

4. TONGUE TWISTERS (Grades 3-8)

A. Purpose: To develop the students ability to use alliteration in writing.

B. Materials: A book of tongue twisters, pencils and paper will be needed.

C. Introduction to the Class: The teacher reads some tongue twisters to the students and the students try to repeat them. The students are to make up their own tongue twisters to share with the class. Lower level students could be given a list of words which all begin with the same letters to give them a start.

1. Sally sells seashells by the seashore.

2. Fuzzy Wuzzy was a bear. Fuzzy Wuzzy had no hair. Fuzzy Wuzzy wasn't fuzzy, Was he?

3. New linoleum

4. Toy boat

5. Peter Piper picked a peck of pickled peppers.

5. FOLK TALES (Grades 3-8)

A. Purpose: To provide practice in creative writing.

B. Materials: A selection of folk tales, paper and pencils will be needed.

C. Introduction to the Class: The teacher selects a couple of folk tales to read to the students. After discussing the idea of folk tales, the teacher reads the beginning of a folk tale to the students. The characters should be introduced and the main idea started when the teacher stops reading. The students are to work in groups of four. The first of the group will write for about ten minutes before passing it to one of the other group members. All four students will add to the story. The new creations should be shared with the rest of the class.

6. "ADD A CHARACTER" (Grades 3-8)

A. Purpose: To provide practice in creative writing using the first person.

B. Materials: A selection of novels with varying reading levels, paper and pencils will be needed.

C. Introduction to the Class: The students are to read a novel and choose their favorite event in the book. They are to rewrite the event adding themselves as a character and writing in the first person. It would be helpful to do this as a class before having the students do it independently. A short story could be used as an introduction to this activity.

7. WRITE A LETTER (Grades 3-8)

A. Purpose: To provide practice in writing to persuade and present a different way to report on a book.

B. Materials: A selection of books, pencils and paper will be needed.

C. Introduction to the Class: Each student is to read a book of his/her choice. The teacher is to review the format of a friendly letter with the class. Each student is to write a letter to a friend trying to encourage the friend to read this book. The letter should include a description of the main characters and information on the major plot.

8. BOOK REPORT FORM (Grades 3-8)

A. Purpose: To provide practice in writing verse as well as stimulate independent reading.

B. Materials: A selection of books, paper and pencils will be needed.

C. Introduction to the Class: Each student is to read a book and then write a poem about it. An example follows:

I read a book named <u>The Enchanted Fawn</u>,
I stayed awake reading almost 'til dawn.
From the enchanted water he did drink,
And a fawn he became, as quick as a wink.

9. INTERVIEW THE AUTHOR (Grades 3-8)

A. Purpose: To encourage critical thinking and give practice in writing.

B. Materials: Provide a selection of novels, paper and pencils.

C. Introduction to the Class: Each student is to read a novel and then write a pretend interview with the author. The interview can be between the student and the author, or between a character in the book and the author. The teacher might supply the students with some suggested questions to give them a start. For example:

1. Where did you get your ideas for writing this book?

2. Did you really live in the...?

3. Do you have a family?

If the student is writing the interview between the author and a character, the character might ask questions like, ''Why did this have to happen?''

10. HOBBIES (Grades 3-8)

A. Purpose: To encourage creative writing.

B. Materials: A selection of books on hobbies, paper and pencils will be needed.

C. Introduction to the Class: The students are instructed to read a book on hobbies and choose a hobby about which to write and share with the class. The students should be encouraged to write about their own hobby, if they have one. If they don't have a hobby, this activity might help them find one.

11. CIRCUS LIFE (Grades 3-8)

A. Purpose: To stimulate independent reading and encourage creative writing.

B. Materials: Provide a selection of stories dealing with the circus. Paper and pencils will also be needed.

C. Introduction to the Class: Each student is to read a circus story. These stories do not have to be long and the same story can be read by many students. The teacher discusses with the class the many circus related occupations. Each student is to pretend he/she is a circus person and write about the circus performance from his/her person's point of view. The many occupations include performers, ringmaster, animal trainers, ticket takers, cooks and concession stand workers.

12. LET'S PRETEND (Grades 3-8)

A. Purpose: To provide practice in creative writing.

B. Materials: A selection of books relating to the zoo, paper and pencils will be needed.

C. Introduction to the Class: Each student is to read a book about the zoo. This book can be fiction or nonfiction. The students are instructed to pretend they are an animal in the zoo. They are to write about one day at the zoo, telling what they are thinking when people come up to look at them and what the people seem to be thinking.

13. FICTION (Grades 3-8)

A. Purpose: To provide practice in writing to persuade.

B. Materials: A selection of fiction books, paper and pencils will be needed.

C. Introduction to the Class: The students are instructed to read a story. Instruct them to write an advertisement for the book and pretend to try to sell it. Then, have the students write a letter to a friend trying to persuade him/her to read the book. Remember to show the main idea, or theme of the story, tell something exciting about the main characters and tell why you think others would like the story. Be careful not to tell the ending.

14. JUST SO STORIES (Grades 3-8)

A. Purpose: To provide for practice in creative writing.

B. Materials: Some ''Just So Stories', paper and pencils will be needed.

C. Introduction to the Class: The teacher should familiarize the students with ''Just So Stories'' by reading some of Kiplings. ''How the Lion Got His Roar'' is a good example. The students are to write a ''Just So Story'' about some animal. The story can be about a real animal or a funny one about a make believe animal made up of parts of several different animals. An example would be ''How the snake grew legs on which to walk''.

15. WRITING A DIARY (Grades 3-8)

A. Purpose: To provide practice in creative writing.

B. Materials: Provide a selection of nonfiction books about animals, paper and pencils.

C. Introduction to the Class: The students are instructed to read about a particular animal. Pay close attention to its habitat, the food it eats and the enemies it has. The students are to write a diary of one day in the life of the animal he/she chooses.

16. AUTOBIOGRAPHY (Grades 3-8)

A. Purpose: To provide experiences in creative writing while learning the meaning of the word, 'autobiography.'

B. Materials: A selection of autobiographies, paper and pencils will be needed.

C. Introduction to the Class: The student is to read an autobiography and write about an early memory in that person's life or a recent memory in that person's life. When this is finished, the students are instructed to write a portion of their own autobiography selecting either an early or a recent memory to discuss.

17. WRITE A MOVIE SCRIPT (Grades 5-8)

A. Purpose: To provide experiences in creative writing.

B. Materials: A selection of good action stories, paper and pencils will be needed.

C. Introduction to the Class: The teacher should read an action story to the class. This can be a short story. The class develops a movie script from the events in the short story. This is written on the board so the students can have an example to follow. The students are instructed to read a story and develop a movie script about the story. This can encompass the whole story or simply dwell on one incident in the story.

18. FAIRY TALES (Grades 3-8)

A. Purpose: To provide experiences with creative writing.

B. Materials: A selection of books containing fairy tales, paper and pencils will be needed.

C. Introduction to the Class: The students are to select a fairy tale to read. They are to rewrite the fairy tale making the hero the villain and the villain the hero. These rewritten fairy tales should be shared with the class.

19. WRITE A STORY (Grades 3-8)

A. Purpose: To provide practice in creative writing.

B. Materials: Provide a selection of short novels at varying reading levels, paper and pencils.

C. Introduction to the Class: Each student selects a book to read. The teacher appoints partners. Each student is to read his/her story and then provide his/her partner with the following information:

1) Name of book

2) Main characters with a description of each one

3) Setting and time of story

4) The problem or action based on the plot

5) A list of 15 vocabulary words from the story (These words should be ones the reader doesn't know or at least doesn't see often.)

The partner is to rewrite the story based on the above information and using as many of the vocabulary words as he can.

20. WRITE A TELEGRAM (Grades 3-8)

A. Purpose: To provide practice in summarizing and being concise.

B. Materials: Provide books, paper and pencils.

C. Introduction to the Class: Each student is to read a story and write a telegram about the story using 20 words or less. The telegram is delivered to his/her partner. The partner is to write a report of the book using only the 20 word telegram and the story title. These reports should be at least 50 words. When this is finished, the partners share the original story and the new one.

21. SELL YOUR BOOK (Grades 3-8)

A. Purpose: To provide practice in writing to persuade.

B. Materials: Provide paper, pencils and a selection of novels.

C. Introduction to the Class: The students are instructed to read a book and then write an advertisement for it. The advertisements should be displayed on the bulletin board. They should include information on where the book can be found and why it is so great!

22. WRITE A TITLE (Grades 3-8)

A. Purpose: To provide practice in summarizing to write a story title.

B. Materials: A collection of children's magazines, articles or newspapers that can be cut, poster board and scissors will be needed.

C. Introduction to the Class: The students are instructed to cut out some short articles and paste them on poster board. The students are to cut off the story title and exchange stories with someone. Each student is to write a title for the stories given to him/her by his/her partner. The partners then share the original title.

KID'S LIT

181 activities to give teachers in grades K-8 ideas to involve students with children's literature while they are learning language arts. There are 29 activities in word recognition, 75 that deal with comprehension, 9 that involve dictionary and reference skills, 22 which help to develop critical thinking skills, 34 which emphasize creative writing skills and 12 which encourage independent reading. Children may be asked, for example, to "Create a Newspaper," using ideas from a book they have read. The newspaper might contain editorials, weather reports, feature stories, historical events, advertisements, etc. The student could pretend to be a main character in the story and use this character in a feature article. The activities are all designed to enchance children's enjoyment and understanding of books.

23. JOB DESCRIPTIONS (Grades 3-8)

A. Purpose: To provide practice in creative writing and to learn about possible occupations.

B. Materials: A selection of fiction or nonfiction books dealing with a variety of occupations, pencils and paper will be needed.

C. Introduction to the Class: The students are instructed to read a book about a particular job in which they are interested. They are to write a job description to share with the rest of the class. Their job description should give the following information:

1) Type of job

2) Location or setting of job

3) Hours to be worked

4) Education required

5) Experience required

6) Vacation allowed

7) Other fringe benefits

24. STORY TITLES (Grades 3-8)

A. Purpose: To provide practice in creative writing as well as in developing imagination.

B. Materials: A selection of books or a list of book titles, pencils and paper will be needed.

C. Introduction to the Class: The students are instructed to use the story titles to construct a sensible story. This is more fun when done in a group. For example, a story might be as follows:

The Boy Next Door was really an All American. He was a Rookie First Baseman and great at everything he tried. He wanted to go on an Incredible Journey...

Most, but not all of the words in the stories, should be story titles.

25. BE AN EXCHANGE STUDENT (Grades 3-8)

A. Purpose: To provide practice in creative writing.

B. Materials: Provide paper, pencils and a selection of novels which have their settings in other countries.

C. Introduction to the Class: Each student is to read a novel. They are to pretend that they are foreign exchange students living in that country. They are instructed to write a letter to their parents or some friends. The letter should consist of impressions or facts of the area in which they are living, as well as tell about how they are feeling living away from home.

26. WRITE AN ENDING (Grades 3-8)

   A. Purpose: To provide practice in creative writing.

   B. Materials: A mystery story, paper and pencils will be needed.

   C. Introduction to the Class: The teacher should select a fairly short mystery story to read to the class. The teacher should read the story aloud up to the point in the plot where the foundation has been laid, and suspense created, but anything can happen. The students are instructed to write the ending. These endings should be shared with the class. The class should vote on the best ending. Then the teacher should read the end of the story from the book.

27. CREATE A NEWSPAPER (Grades 5-6)

   A. Purpose: To give students a chance to write newspaper articles and to develop creative writing skills.

   B. Materials: Paper and pencils will be needed. Before this activity is used, the entire class is to have read a particular book.

C. Introduction to the Class: The children are to create a newspaper using the main topic or ideas from the book that was read. The newspaper might contain editorials, weather reports, feature stories, historical events, advertisements, drawing or just about anything one might see in a newspaper. In feature stories, a student can pretend to be the main character or take the part of the protagonist or antagonist of the story. If the book read was a historical one, the newspaper could contain headlines or advertisements pertaining to that era. The newspaper is beneficial because it gives a variety of experiences in writing of different types. It also helps children understand a story better by looking at it from another person's point of view.

Zoo to spruce up its elephant house

Ruth, Kita to get new pool

By James L. Kerwin
News Staff Writer

Among the oldest tenants of the Detroit Zoo, elephants Ruth and Kita finally are getting some respect from their landlord.

Their quarters, which hark back to the early 1930s, are in shambles.

The interior is drab and dreary. Exterior walls made from gunite are peeling away. The roof leaks, the plumbing leaves them standing in smelly water, and new electric wiring is needed.

Conditions are so bad they can't even have visitors from the among the thousands who drop by the zoo each day to view the wildlife exhibits.

But a major renovation has begun to correct the deficiencies, and add a few new features — improved landscaping, a flight cage with exotic birds to keep company with the aging pachyderms, new display graphics that tells visitors all about Asian elephants and an indoor pool to help them keep tidy and cool.

28. BIOGRAPHIES (Grades 3-5)

A. **Purpose:** To learn how to write biographies.

B. **Materials:** Provide paper, crayons, pencils, cardboard and old magazines.

C. **Introduction to the Class:** Provide a table in the room to display the above mentioned materials. Each of the children must select a partner with whom to work. Each partner is to interview the other and then write a biography of his or her partner. Using the materials above, each partner will construct a book. The cardboard serves as a book cover and the old magazines provide the illustrations. Illustrations could also be done with pencils and crayons. The biographies should be shared with the class.

29. COMPLETE A STORY (Grades 3-6)

A. **Purpose:** To develop the students' creative writing skills.

B. **Materials:** A selection of short stories, paper and pencils will be needed.

C. **Introduction to the Class:** Choose a short story to read to the students. Read the first part of the story to them. Stop at a point when they seem to be well involved in the plot. They are then instructed to finish the story. This could also be done by reading the last half of the story and asking them to write the beginning.

30. CHANGE A STORY (Grades 2-4)

A. Purpose: To provide practice in creative writing.

B. Materials: Provide the book <u>Nothing Ever Happens On My Block</u>, by Ellen Raskin, pencils, paper and crayons or markers.

C. Introduction to the Class: Read the book to the class. Talk about the characters and the setting. Divide the class into groups of six. One member of each group draws a slip of paper out of a box. On the slips of paper, one of the following should have been printed.

1. Change the story so it fits the title, <u>Nothing Ever Happens On My Farm</u>.

2. Change the story so it fits the title, <u>Nothing Ever Happens In My Zoo</u>.

3. Change the story so it fits the title, <u>Nothing Ever Happens In My School</u>.

4. Change the story using an elephant to tell the story.

5. Change the story using a kitten to tell the story. (Any animal can be used).

6. Change the story using the current United States President to tell the story.

7. Change the story, using George Washington to tell the story. (Any famous person can be used).

Have the groups share their newly-written stories with the class.

31. WRITE A STORY (Grades K-3)

A. Purpose: To develop the student's creative thinking skills.

B. Materials: Story film strips, a slide projector, shelf paper and crayons or felt tip markers will be needed.

C. Introduction to the Class: The children should have seen several film strips of stories before attempting this activity. The teacher provides the text by reading the words printed on the frames or using the corresponding record. A new filmstrip is introduced and the children are told that it's their turn to be story- tellers. They are to make up the story as the slides are seen on the screen. The children take turns telling the story by looking at each picture frame and saying whatever comes to mind. The teacher should write the story as it unfolds. This process can be repeated on different days and the stories compared. The story can be illustrated and put on the wall for display.

32. AUTOBIOGRAPHIES (Grades 2-5)

A. Purpose: To write your autobiography.

B. Materials: Provide paper, pencils, magazines and glue.

C. Introduction to the Class: The children are instructed to draw a picture of themselves at age one, age two, age three and continue to whatever age they are at present. Explain that they should show themselves doing something or depicting an important event in their lives at each age. Older children are instructed to write captions for their pictures. Their pictures are compiled into a book making their autobiography. Provide magazines for children who do not like to draw. Magazine pictures can be used instead of drawing to depict events in their lives. Depicting these concrete experiences should give children a more complete understanding of what an autobiography is and how it can be written.

33. REWRITE THE TITLES (Grades 3-5)

A. Purpose: To give practice in using synonyms.

B. Materials: Dictionaries, paper and pencils will be needed.

C. Introduction to the Class: The teacher writes the names of some books on the chalkboard. The children are to rewrite the titles using synonyms in place of the words underlined. A sample list follows:

The <u>Hostile Beaches</u>	The Unfriendly Seashores
I Have Just <u>Begun</u> to <u>Fight</u>	I Have Just Started to Oppose
The <u>Fortune Road</u>	The Riches Street
The <u>Darkness</u> and the <u>Dawn</u>	The Blackness and the Morning
<u>Little Women</u>	Tiny Ladies
The <u>Black Cauldron</u>	The Dark Pot
April <u>Morning</u>	April Dawn
<u>War</u> and <u>Peace</u>	Battle and Freedom

34. CREATING A STORY (Grades 3-5)

A. Purpose: To use a given set of words to write a story.

B. Materials: A selection of picture books will be needed.

C. Introduction to the Class: Each child is given a picture book and is instructed to write down two words from the story which have more than five letters. The teacher writes all of these words on the chalkboard and the children take

turns reading a word. The teacher uses two of the words in
a sentence to begin a story and the children take turns adding sentences to the story. They must use, at least, two of
the words in one sentence. When the story is finished, several
children should read it in its entirety.

UNIT VI
ENCOURAGING INDEPENDENT READING

1. COMPARE YOUR ADVENTURES (Grades 3-8)

A. Purpose: To encourage independent reading.

B. Materials: A selection of novels, paper and pencils will be needed.

C. Introduction to the Class: The students are to select a story about a character who is much like himself or herself. The students are to write about an adventure they had that was like their main character's adventure. The students are to tell in what ways the two adventures were alike and in what ways they were different.

Character's Adventure	My Adventure

Similarities

1.
2.
3.

Differences

1.
2.
3.

2. COMIC BOOKS (Grades 3-8)

A. Purpose: To challenge the uninspired reader.

B. Materials: Provide comic books and business envelopes.

C. Introduction to the Class: Cut and separate the squares of a comic book episode. Put all of the squares of one story in one envelope. The student is to arrange the comic in the correct sequence. This can be done independently or shared with the whole class. The newspaper comic section can also be used for this activity.

3. BUILD A MOBILE (K-8)

A. Purpose: To encourage independent reading.

B. Materials: Provide a selection of books, construction paper, crayons, markers, colored pencils, string and glue.

C. Introduction to the Class: The students are to read a book, specifically to "know" the characters. The students are to make a mobile to hang from the ceiling which represents four or five charcters in their book. The following example shows Tom represented as a football, Ted, a bicycle, and Susi a happy face. The things on the mobile should show something of the charcter's personality or interests.

TITLE

4. MAKE A SCRAP BOOK (K-8)

A. Purpose: To encourage independent reading.

B. Materials: Provide magazines to cut, a selection of books, construction paper, scissors, glue, markers and crayons.

C. Introduction to the Class: The students are to read a book and then make a scrap book of things related to the book. These can be pictures cut from magazines, illustrations done by the students themselves or materials picked up outside (such as leaves, twigs, etc.).

5. WHERE HAVE YOU BEEN? (Grades 3-8)

A. Purpose: To encourage outside reading.

B. Materials: Paper, pencils, and nonfiction books or pamphlets on particular places will be needed.

C. Introduction to the Class: The students are asked to read a book about a place they have been. These can be library books or materials obtained through writing the Chamber of Commerce of whatever state is selected. After reading, they are to write a pretend letter to a friend convincing him to visit this wonderful place.

6. SHARING BOOKS THROUGH ART (Grades K-8)

A. Purpose: To motivate independent reading through art.

B. Materials: General art supplies will be needed.

C. Introduction to the Class: Each student is to make a book jacket for his book. The book jackets are displayed around the room after the reader tells the class a little about his book. The book jackets can be done with a variety of art supplies. The book jacket should have a summary included on the inside of the front cover, just as real book jackets do. The back flap should have some information on the author. After completing his book jacket, the student tries to sell his book to his friends by displaying and discussing his book jacket.

7. PANTOMIME (Grades 3-8)

A. Purpose: To motivate outside reading.

B. Materials: A selection of novels at varying reading levels will be needed.

C. Introduction to the Class: Each student reads a novel. The teacher writes the name of several novels on the board. Each student is to pantomime a scene from the book. The rest of the class is to guess the book title and tell why a particular title was chosen.

8. CLASS RECORDS (Grades 3-8)

A. Purpose: To make a class file for summaries of books the students have read.

B. Materials: Provide books, 3 x 5 cards, a card file and pencils.

C. Introduction to the Class: The students are to fill out a summary card on the books they read. The card should tell the author and the title. It should also have a summary of the book and tell whether the reader liked the book. Other students can use this file to select something that interests them.

```
Title:
Author:
Summary:
```

9. KEEP A RECORD (Grades 1-4)

A. Purpose: To keep a record of books read and to motivate an interest in reading.

B. Materials: Colored construction paper will be needed.

C. Introduction to the Class: Make a tree on a bulletin board without any leaves. Also, cut out leaves to be attached later. Each time a student finishes a book, he/she takes a leaf and writes the name of the book on it. The whole class will enjoy watching the tree add leaves as more and more books are read.

10. PLAYS (Grades 3-8)

A. Purpose: To provide extended activites with plays to encourage independent reading.

B. Materials: Provide a selection of books of plays, art materials and cardboard for setting.

C. Introduction to the Class: The class is divided into groups of four. Four students read the same play. They are instructed to (1) Choose a character in the play to depict. This can be done by either planning a costume to wear or drawing the costume remembering the time and setting of the play. (2) Prepare a stage setting for the major acts of the play using large pieces of cardboard, paints and a varie-ty of art materials. (3) Present the play or, at least a scene in the play. The class may decide which of the plays would be fun to perform for their parents or fellow students.

11. ILLUSTRATIONS (Grades 3-8)

A. Purpose: To provide students with practice in using pictures to help in comprehension and to motivate further reading.

B. Materials: Provide library books, pencils, drawing paper, colored chalk, markers or paints.

C. Introduction to the Class: The teacher selects a picture book which has numerous pictures that help to tell the story in the book. The class looks at the pictures sequentially and together they write the story the pictures tell. The teacher writes this on the board. After developing the picture story and rereading it, the teacher reads the entire book. The students are given drawing paper and colored chalk to illustrate their own book. They should write the title, the author and the illustrator on the bottom of their picture.

12. MAKE A BOOKMARK (K-8)

A. Purpose: To encourage independent reading.

B. Materials: Provide a selection of books, poster board, crayons and marking pens.

C. Introduction to the Class: The students are to select a book to read. They are to make a bookmark to give to a classmate. The bookmark should tell the title of the book and should illustrate an interesting scene in the book.

FOR TEACHER NOTES

FOR TEACHER NOTES

FOR TEACHER NOTES

FOR TEACHER NOTES

FOR TEACHER NOTES

FOR TEACHER NOTES

FOR TEACHER NOTES

FOR TEACHER NOTES

FOR TEACHER NOTES

FOR TEACHER NOTES

THINKING OF A GIFT TO OPEN A CHILD'S IMAGINATION THROUGH A READING DISCOVERY STORYBOOK?

HITCHHIKER ON THE WIND offers 85 pages of exciting reading. It is a story about Jim and his meeting with Archy, a mouse of very unusual talents. Children of all ages will enjoy the relationship that Jim builds with Archy. We all must learn to live with our limitations and yet challenge ourselves to the maximum and this is the idea behind the story that Greg and Rosemae Hafstrom have written.

001-3 HITCHHIKER ON THE WIND $6.95

DRAMA-PAK™

Each "Pak" contains a playbook for each main character and one for the director.

SCHOOL FOR ANGELS
A Fantasy · by Natalie Bovee Hutson
Six Main Characters

Less than one week until Christmas and chaos reigns in The Great Beyond! While Earth bombards the Heavenly Headmaster with urgent requests for "perfect" angels, it is discovered that the current "crop" is woefully lacking in "angel skills". Cherubs have been playing frisbee with the stars, conducting pillow fights with the clouds, and swinging from the Pearly Gates. The angel choir doesn't even know the words to "Silent Night"!

A delightful play for all ages and all seasons.

☐ 304-7. . . . . $9.95

THE GRUMBLE GROUP
A Comedy · by Natalie Bovee Hutson
Five Characters

The Grumble Group meets regularly (and grudgingly) at a city bus stop, where they find endless subjects about which to complain. On the surface these four individuals appear to be cantankerous old-timers, finding nothing right with the world. But as they reveal themselves to the audience, and through the help of an optimistic newcomer, it slowly becomes apparent that beneath the somewhat comic exteriors, lie sensitive people who have, for various reasons, become quite disenchanted with life.

A good choice for all ages.

☐ 301-2. . . . . $9.95

ME, BETH CONNORS
A Teenage Drama · by Natalie Bovee Hutson
Seven Characters

Meet Beth Connors, an average twelve-year-old, who through a series of flashbacks, takes the audience by the hand and leads them through a typical day in her life. It's a day filled with girlish giggling, a mysterious phone call, and the usual scraps with a pesky younger brother. But best of all, it is a day in which a routine visit to her grandmother in a nursing home, enables Beth to view life in a more adult manner.

☐ 303-9. . . . . $9.95

DRAMA-PAK™

Each "Pak" contains a playbook for each main characters and one for the director.

MR. TEDLEY'S TREEHOUSE
A Drama for the Young - by Natalie Bovee Hutson
Seven Characters

Mr. Tedley is a child's dream come true. He lives alone in a treehouse surviving on berries and nuts, offering friendship and vast knowledge to the younger set. But is he real? Ryan and Joey know that he is, but cannot convince others of the fact, and this troubles them.

In a simplistic way, the play deals with every child's need to fantasize and cling to dreams. Yet it also emphasizes that there comes a time when one must leave the fantasies behind and face the real world.

A charming play for young and old.

☐ **302-0** **$9.95**

THE READING OF THE WILL
A Farce - by Natalie Bovee Hutson
Seven Characters

Henry P. Jaybody may be deceased, but he is not absent from the reading of his will! Knowing that his greedy heirs would do their best to "out-mourn" each other, Henry had the foresight to plan a scene which would send the tribe in all directions, showing their true colors - and practically trampling one another in the process.

An action-filled play with characters who are fun to portray and even funnier to watch.

☐ **305-5** **$9.95**

THE WRONGFUL CLAIM
An Old-Fashioned Melodrama - by Natalie Bovee Hutson
Eight Characters

The lovely and innocent Melody Lark is but a servant in the home of wealthy Vanessa Vapors. Vanessa's avaricious daughter, Crystal, is envious of Melody's childlike charm and attentions of the gardener, Barnaby Barnhart. So when Crystal accidentally discovers that Melody is about to fall heir to a fortune, she plots her disinheritance. Unaware of his sister's scheme, an equally greedy Humphrey Vapors devises his own plot to discredit Melody.

An old-fashioned melodrama with lots of heroes and villains and a chance to hiss, boo, and applaud them all.

☐ **300-4** **$9.95**

TABLETMASTERS™

Duplicator Masters
You Tear from a Tablet!

- Faster to Use
- Easier to Handle
- Flat-Stacking

and only.......

$3⁹⁵ each

Factual Recall

	Grade	Cat. No.
Helps the student make use of pictures and words in a fact-finding experience, using detailed recall and supportive visual evidence. Excellent diagnostic tool for determining comprehension and ability to relate observation to written questions.	1	603-8
	2	607-0
	3	611-9

Following Directions

	Grade	Cat. No.
Provides realistic drills necessary to teach students the processes of reading, understanding, and then following directions. Each worksheet has a number of directions, each of which must be completed progressively. Verbal instructions may be added.	1	604-6
	2	608-9
	3	612-7

Thinking Skills

	Grade	Cat. No.
Study sheets call for visual sequencing, reasoning, classifying, and using cause and effect thinking skills. Sharpens each student's ability to draw conclusions, and their reasoning should be explained before answers are accepted or rejected.	1	605-4
	2	609-7
	3	613-5

Vocabulary Development

	Grade	Cat. No.
Promotes word-building through usage, exploration, similarities, expressive language and identification. Matching pictures and words reinforces the relationship between the two. A range of descriptive words, synonyms, antonyms and other forms is used.	1	606-2
	2	610-0
	3	614-3

80584

DUPLICATOR BOOKS

Use our ideas in duplicator form to cut teacher preparation time and fulfill the needs for supplementary activities in the following areas of study:

ONLY $6.95 Each

LANGUAGE ARTS
- ☐ **ED501-5 SPICE VOL. I** — K-2
- ☐ **ED502-3 SPICE VOL. II** — 2-4
- ☐ **ED505-8 ANCHOR VOL. I** — 4-6
- ☐ **ED506-6 ANCHOR VOL. II** — 6-8
- ☐ **ED564-3 PHONICS VOL. I** — K-2
- ☐ **ED565-1 PHONICS VOL. II** — 2-4
- ☐ **ED567-8 GRAMMAR VOL. I** — 4-6
- ☐ **ED568-6 GRAMMAR VOL. II** — 6-8
- ☐ **ED509-0 RESCUE VOL. I** — K-4
  (Remedial Reading)
- ☐ **ED516-3 FLAIR VOL. I** — 3-8
  (Creative Writing)
- ☐ **ED527-9 DICTIONARY VOL. I** — K-2
  (Single Letters)
- ☐ **ED528-7 DICTIONARY VOL. II** — K-2
  (Blends)
- ☐ **ED529-5 DICTIONARY VOL. III** — 3-6
- ☐ **ED530-9 DICTIONARY VOL. IV** — 7-9
- ☐ **ED537-6 LIBRARY VOL. I** — 3-6
- ☐ **ED538-4 LIBRARY VOL. II** — 7-9

MUSIC
- ☐ **ED561-9 NOTE VOL. I** — K-2
- ☐ **ED562-7 NOTE VOL. II** — 3-6

EARLY LEARNING
- ☐ **ED512-0 LAUNCH VOL. I**
  (Basic Readiness)
- ☐ **ED513-9 LAUNCH VOL. II**
  (Additional Skills)

MATHEMATICS
- ☐ **ED533-3 PLUS VOL. I** — K-2
- ☐ **ED534-1 PLUS VOL. II** — 2-4
- ☐ **ED523-6 CHALLENGE VOL. I** — 4-6
- ☐ **ED524-4 CHALLENGE VOL. II** — 6-8

SCIENCE
- ☐ **ED546-5 PROBE VOL. I** — K-2
- ☐ **ED547-3 PROBE VOL. II** — 2-4
- ☐ **ED550-3 INQUIRE VOL. I** — 4-8

SOCIAL STUDIES
- ☐ **ED553-8 SPARK VOL. I** — K-2
- ☐ **ED554-6 SPARK VOL. II** — 2-4

★ ★

ONLY $4.50 Each

EXCLUSIVE WORD LISTS
Each book contains a graded word list — from 738 words at Level 1 to 4,325 words at Level 6.

"Work with Words" Duplicator Books Develop and Reinforce Language Skills on 6 Levels!

A creative new series from the publishers of Spice! Here's a fresh and dynamic approach to teaching and reinforcing language skills. Each master is clearly identified as to the learning objective: recognizing sounds, visual identification, word recognition, word usage, spelling, alphabetizing, word meaning, and so on. Thus the teacher can locate just the right activity at just the right time! To top if off, each book contains our exclusive and previously unpublished graded word list for that level. Each 8½ × 11" book has teacher's guide; 20 masters. Use with any basal program to extend learning through skill-building activities.

☑ **ED262-8** Level 1A	738 words	☐ **ED268-7** Level 4A	2970 words
☐ **ED263-6** Level 1B	738 words	☐ **ED269-5** Level 4B	2970 words
☐ **ED264-4** Level 2A	1416 words	☐ **ED270-9** Level 5A	3613 words
☐ **ED265-2** Level 2B	1416 words	☐ **ED271-7** Level 5B	3613 words
☐ **ED266-0** Level 3A	2303 words	☐ **ED272-5** Level 6A	4325 words
☐ **ED267-9** Level 3B	2303 words	☐ **ED273-3** Level 6B	4325 words

☐ **WWP-500** Complete Set of all 12 books above $54.00

Note: "B" level books are slightly more advanced than "A" level.

Duplicators and idea-books (shown on opposite side) are available at the leading school supply dealers. Ask for them by name.

For a current catalog, contact the publisher.

IDEA-BOOKS FOR ELEMENTARY SCHOOL TEACHERS

Each book was created to meet teachers' needs for simple and explicit ideas to enrich the many subject areas presented to their students.

ONLY $6⁹⁵ Each

LANGUAGE ARTS

- ☐ **ED101-X SPICE** — Primary Language Arts ● Grades K-4
- ☐ **ED109-5 ANCHOR** — Intermediate Language Arts ● Grades 4-8
- ☐ **ED128-1 RESCUE** — Primary Remedial Reading ● Grades K-4
- ☐ **ED112-5 FLAIR** — Creative Writing ● Grades K-8
- ☐ **ED122-2 SCRIBE** — Handwriting ● Grades K-8
- ☐ **ED126-5 PRESS** — Newspaper Activities ● Grades K-8
- ☐ **ED130-3 PHONICS** — Primary Phonics ● Grades K-4
- ☐ **ED134-6 GRAMMAR** — Intermediate Grammar ● Grades 4-8
- ☐ **ED131-1 LISTEN** — Listening Activities ● Grades K-8
- ☐ **ED133-8 VIDEO** — Television Activities ● Grades K-8
- ☐ **ED136-2 REFLECT** — Creative Thought ● Grades 4-Adult
- ☐ **ED137-0 VALUES** — Values Clarification ● Grades K-8
- ☐ **ED139-7 KID'S LIT** — Reading Through Lit ● Grades K-8
- ☐ **ED141-9 LIB. STUDIES** — Library Skills ● Grades K-9

MATHEMATICS & SCIENCE

- ☐ **ED103-6 PLUS** — Primary Mathematics ● Grade K-4
- ☐ **ED116-8 CHALLENGE** — Intermediate Mathematics ● Grades 4-8
- ☐ **ED118-4 METER** — Metrics ● Grades K-8
- ☐ **ED102-8 PROBE** — Primary Science ● Grades K-4
- ☐ **ED121-4 INQUIRE** — Intermediate Science ● Grades 4-8
- ☐ **ED140-0 NATURE** — Outdoor Education ● Grades K-8

SOCIAL STUDIES

- ☐ **ED104-4 SPARK** — Primary Social Studies ● Grades K-4
- ☐ **ED125-7 FOCUS** — Intermediate Social Studies ● Grades 4-8
- ☐ **ED120-6 CHOICE** — Economics ● Grades K-8
- ☐ **ED123-0 CAREER** — Career Education ● Grades K-8
- ☐ **ED135-4 COMPASS** — Map Skills ● Grades K-8

SPECIALTY STUDIES

- ☐ **ED111-7 LAUNCH** — Preschool and Kindergarten Readiness
- ☐ **ED127-3 HOLIDAY** — Holiday Art ● Grades K-8
- ☐ **ED105-2 CREATE** — Primary Art ● Grades K-4
- ☐ **ED124-9 CRAFT** — Intermediate Art ● Grades 4-8
- ☐ **ED113-3 NOTE** — Music ● Grades K-8
- ☐ **ED119-2 GROWTH** — Health ● Grades K-8
- ☐ **ED115-X PREVENT** — Safety ● Grades K-8
- ☐ **ED107-9 STAGE** — Dramatics ● Grades K-8
- ☐ **ED106-0 ACTION** — Physical Education ● Grades K-6
- ☐ **ED117-6 DISPLAY** — Bulletin Board Ideas

Address: ☐ Home   ☐ School (Preferred)

Name ____

Address ____

____

City _________________________ State _________ Zip _________

Idea-books and duplicators (shown on the opposite side) are available at leading school supply dealers or Educational Service, Inc., PO Box 219, Stevensville, Michigan 49127 **1-800-253-0763.**

82586